My Confrontation *with* HELL

Real Demonic Encounters of an Exorcist

MSGR. STEPHEN J. ROSSETTI

Scripture texts in this work are taken from the *New American Bible, revised edition* ©
2010, 1991, 1986, 1970 Confraternity of Christian Doctrine, Washington, D.C. and are
used by permission of the copyright owner. All Rights Reserved. No part of the New
American Bible may be reproduced in any form without permission in writing from the
copyright owner.

Excerpts from the English translation of the *Catechism of the Catholic Church* for use in
the United States of America Copyright © 1994, United States Catholic Conference, Inc.
-- Libreria Editrice Vaticana. Used with Permission. English translation of the *Catechism of
the Catholic Church*: Modifications from the Editio Typica copyright © 1997, United States
Conference of Catholic Bishops—Libreria Editrice Vaticana.

Prayers from "Catholic Handbook of Prayers for Spiritual Liberation and Exorcisms with
Redactor's Notes," 1st ed., and 2nd ed., The University of Santo Tomas Publishing House,
Manila, Philippines" used with permission.

Prayers adapted from Fr. Jose Francisco C. Syquia, "Catholic Handbook of Deliverance
Prayers," Rev. ed. with 12 new prayers, Makati City, PI: St. Pauls Philippines, used
with permission.

Nihil Obstat:
Reverend Monsignor Charles Pope
Censor Deputatus

Imprimatur:
Most Reverend Juan Esposito, J.C.D.
Vicar General and Moderator of the Curia

The Roman Catholic Archdiocese of Washington

March 4, 2025

The *nihil obstat* and *imprimatur* are official declarations that a book or pamphlet is free of
doctrinal or moral error. There is no implication that those who have granted the *nihil
obstat* and the *imprimatur* agree with the content, opinions or statements expressed therein.

*To St. Michael the Archangel
and the Powers of Heaven—
our faithful companions
in the battle against Evil.*

Contents

Introduction

I STARTED IN THIS MINISTRY OF EXORCISM ALMOST TWO DECADES AGO. At that time, there were very few exorcists in the USA or anywhere around the world. There were no training programs and few reliable resources available. I was fortunate, and I believe it was providential, that I "bumped into" one of the only senior exorcists in the USA, who was willing to help me get started. I am grateful to him!

Even today, few seminaries broach the subject with its future priests. This is a serious problem. Within the first few months of ordination, it is common that someone will come to a new priest and say, "Father, I have demons. I need help!" Then, caught unawares and untrained, he is forced to scramble to find out what to do. I get more than a few calls from panicked priests who don't know how to respond.

I never would have expected to finish out my years as a priest as an exorcist, and a VERY busy one at that. Moreover, I have become somewhat of a well-known public figure, in some Catholic circles. This is also quite a surprise. I am by nature a private, introverted person. I now have over 250K followers on social media and the number is steadily rising. They say if you want to make God laugh, tell Him your plans! So much for my quiet retirement.

But I feel very blessed by it all. My great joy is ministering side-by-side with wonderful, faith-filled people. And I am richly blessed by witnessing and assisting the afflicted, formerly in the grasp of Satan, to find liberation. Their faces tell the story. What previously was a face full of angst, despair and torment, now radiates a newfound peace. What was a life filled with despair is replaced by a newfound hope, sometimes even joy! Thanks be to God!

In this ministry, we are daily privileged to experience the truths of the Faith. All that the Church teaches does not remain on an abstract theological level, but gets incarnated very directly in the spiritual combat. We experience the Communion of Saints and Angels, as they come to our aid in casting out Satan and his minions. We see the power of the Church: its priesthood, sacraments and sacramentals. We sprinkle the demons with holy water and hold up a crucifix, and they howl in agony. The Evil One is completely undone by the beautiful Mother of Jesus, whom we dare to call our Mother, too. And many more bedrock teachings of the Church come to life in an exorcism.

In the history of the Church, theological truths were codified in the wake of the experiences of the followers of Jesus. When I started in this ministry, there were few guideposts to follow. The introduction, or *praenotanda*, to the Rite of Exorcism had a few instructions but they were rather general. Now, in today's church, we are in the midst of the codification of the details of this exorcism and deliverance ministry. We have learned much; there is much more to learn.

It is interesting and noteworthy that in whatever country I travel and participate in an exorcism, the foundational truths are common across boundaries. When I sit down with exorcists from other countries, our experiences are more similar than different. We have much in common. Moreover, if one researches the details of exorcisms in past centuries, they are not dissimilar to ours hundreds of years later. The basic "bones" are the same.

This should not come as a surprise. Demons are the same down through the centuries and across national borders. The consistency of our experiences also affirms the truths of what we experience and now pass on to those learning the ministry.

I offer a word of caution. This ministry is not a video game or a Hollywood movie. The stakes are real; they are high; and Satan does not play fair. While the exorcist-priest and his team have many spiritual safeguards, it is imperative to conduct oneself with integrity, operate strictly within the truths of our faith, and within the proper guidelines of this ministry. Sadly, I know of more than a few, including several exorcists, who strayed with disastrous results.

In this book, I have simply shared my experiences. Some may take exception. Fair enough. Much of what I have written is not *de fide* but rather the experience of one exorcist and I am very much open to disagreement.

Toward the end of the book, I am particularly pleased to offer the first-hand experiences of three courageous individuals who personally suffered under the torments of Satan and want to share their stories with you. These stories give the reader a chance to walk with them through the darkness and torments of demonic afflictions, as they struggle to find hope and new life. This is a unique addition and a special grace for us.

These recent years in this exorcism ministry have been "quite a ride." We can complain that Hollywood often exaggerates and over-dramatizes reality. But I can say that at times, the truth and our experiences are more dramatic and more hair-raising than Hollywood can imagine. Perhaps it is because we are operating from an experiential contact with Evil, which is more hideous, and more lethal than any movie can depict.

At the same time, Hollywood has difficulty grasping the power of grace, the beauty of Mary and the heavenly court, the sacrifice of Jesus, the majesty of the Church, and the overwhelming love of God. In addition to being regularly slimed by demons, we are more often buoyed up and transformed by love and grace.

Perhaps unexpectedly, I would say that the one abiding experience of this ministry and our God is that of joy. Joy permeates our team and its ministry. Joy radiates in our words and actions. Joy radiates from our faces. Who would expect joy to be found in such a place as an exorcism? On the contrary, I would say: "If joy is not present, is the power of Christ really being made present?"

Joy is an irrepressible sign of the Holy Spirit and it is this Spirit that animates our work.

Blacker than Black, Horrifying Beyond Description

"WHEN YOU SEE THE DEMONS," I ASKED HER, "WHAT DO THEY LOOK LIKE?" She answered, "They are blacker than black and ugly beyond description. Horror movies do not come close to how awful they are." I asked her to describe them in more detail and she said: "The demons were distorted and misshapen. Some had claws instead of hands; others had horns; some had tails. If they had two eyes or any recognizable limbs, they were malformed. These demons were all like naked, ugly, vicious animals. Most of them did not have bodies; they were just black shapeless forms." Allie has a "charism" of actually seeing demons, which we have verified many times, and I have no doubt that her description is true.

I heard the following story, which I cannot verify, but it has a ring of truth to me. A woman prayed to see the demon that was assigned by Satan over a large city. (Every city and country have an angel assigned by God. Satan mimics and inverts God's actions; he assigns a demon to each city and country as well.) Her request, although likely inappropriate, was granted and the vision was so horrifying that she had a heart attack and ended up in the hospital. Many people claim to see demons but, if they do, they don't really have a direct vision of them. If they saw demons in their true selves, it might be more than they could bear, as this woman found out. Allie has a special charism from God to see them, a grace that she did not request. And she has the important grace of protection to withstand such an awful sight.

The reason demons are so hideous is that every sin is hideous and an offense against our all-loving and infinitely holy God. We humans really do not grasp the awful, infinitely-offending nature of sins, even our "little" ones. In reality, there are no "little" sins. One common experience of the great mystics is how awful their sins are and that they truly deserve to go to hell, were it not for the great gift of salvation in Christ. For example, before St. Gemma received the stigmata, God humbled her by showing her a true glimpse of the evil of her sins. She wrote: "All of a sudden... I felt an interior sorrow for my sins far deeper than I had ever experienced before. In fact, it brought me very, very close to death... My intellect could think of nothing but my sins and the offense they gave to God."[1]

As such, sin and demons are ugly beyond all telling. In our ministry of exorcism, we occasionally experience the ugliness of hell. For example, in the midst of one exorcism session, one of the priests arrived late. He entered the room and said, "What is that awful smell?" He said there was a horrible odor of death and decay in the room. Similarly, in Allie's vision of hell she said, "The smell ... was atrocious. It made me want to throw up." Likewise, St. Faustina said in her vision of hell there was a "continual darkness and a terrible suffocating smell."[2]

Seeing demons, and especially Satan himself, is one of the greatest sufferings of hell. St. Faustina said that one of the seven sufferings of hell is the vision of Satan. "How terribly ugly Satan is!... Just the sight of him is more disgusting than all the torments of hell."[3] In *The Dialogue*, St. Catherine of Siena wrote that she would "rather walk on a road of fire even until the Day of Judgment than to see [Satan] again."[4]

When Allie first started seeing demons, she said one of the things that struck her was their complete lack of remorse or compassion. They simply do not have a drop of care for anyone else. They are malignant, violent narcissists and actually enjoy inflicting pain on others and making them suffer. As such, they are complete sadists.

I am stunned and dismayed by young people who are putting tattoos of demons on their bodies. One young man who came for help, who was having demonic attacks, had a tattoo of a demon on his hip. I asked him why he did that and he responded, "I thought it would make me a better person." Astounding!?!

When Halloween approaches, I am typically asked by parents if it is okay to have their children participate. I do not like to be a killjoy and I enjoy a good celebration. However, I caution them against dressing their children up to be devils, witches, skeletons or any other depiction of evil. After reading St. Faustina's description of hell, why would anyone clothe their beloved children in demonic images? We trivialize the true horrid nature of sin, evil and demons. Rather, I recommend they dress their children up in images of holiness. One faithful Catholic couple had their children choose their favorite saints and then dressed them up as such.

In our post-Christian society today, there is increasing inversion of the Truth, which is a tactic of the Evil One. People say what is evil is actually good and they believe that which is truly good to be evil. I get frustrated with it all and I half-jokingly tell people: "I want to give the following one-minute homily at a Sunday Mass: Let's get down to the basics. God is good. Satan is bad. Angels are good. Demons are bad. Satan is not your friend!" These basic truths were taken for granted just a few years ago. Today, they are not.

Demons of Fatigue and Depression

WHEN WE BEGAN THE SESSION, I WAS FEELING FINE. However, halfway through the exorcism, I felt as if all of my strength was gone. I could barely move or speak. I had to force myself to say the prayers. Then the possessed person likewise said, "I am feeling very, very tired." "This is strange," I thought, "What is happening?" Then it occurred to me—it's demonic. So, I commanded the "demons of fatigue" to depart. I said it again and again: "Demons of fatigue, in the Holy Name of Jesus I command you to leave!" Eventually, the fatigue lifted and we both returned to the task at hand.

This is yet another demonic trick. They try all sorts of things to stop an exorcism. This particular ruse is subtle. You would never think of demons being able to make you feel so tired you cannot move.

Similarly, not long ago, a layman complained to me that whenever he tries to work at his ministry, he is overwhelmed with an uncharacteristic tiredness. It saps his energy and he can barely function. It was very diagnostic that the tiredness only came over this energetic person when he began his ministry. I suspected a demonic cause and told him so. I suggested he use holy water liberally over himself and his workplace, and also begin his ministry with daily deliverance prayers. After deliverance prayers being said, he is now able to work without abnormal fatigue.

Sharing this experience with others in the exorcism ministry, I found out it was rather common. One new exorcist called me on the phone and asked my advice. "I don't understand," he said, "but I get incredibly tired just doing one or two exorcism sessions." I explained to him that the presence of demons saps the energy of the afflicted person and perhaps even the Exorcist. Sometimes I have to force myself to continue with the prayers, as if I am trying to walk through quicksand.

A common expression is: "You cannot give what you don't have." Satan and his dark world have no life, no joy, no happiness, and no life-giving energy. Their world is hopeless, despairing and depressive. This is a great mistake for those who bargain with Satan. They often think Satan will give them great gifts, but he cannot give what he does not have. He cannot make someone love you; real love is from God. He cannot give you any peace or life-giving energy or happiness; he does not have any. When Satan touches something or someone, it saps the life and energy from it, and it eventually dies.

I have been praying over a woman who practiced witchcraft for years. It has been a long, arduous battle but she is getting much better. The main symptom of the presence of demons is a depression and darkness that hangs over her. It became worse and worse as she delved more deeply, year after year, into the occult. It was becoming debilitating. When we began the exorcism sessions, you could see the darkness and heaviness in her eyes and entire demeanor. But by the end of each session, it was beginning to lift and you could see the life returning to her face. While she is not completely free, the fatigue, depression and darkness are slowly lifting and she is finding more joy and peace in her life.

Most bouts of exhaustion have physiological and/ or psychological roots, but sometimes they have a demonic origin. I am most suspicious when it occurs in the midst of an exorcism or when it occurs unexpectedly as a person begins a holy task. When demons desperately don't want something to happen, this is one of their subtle tricks.

Baphomet Threatens An Exorcist

Baphomet, a high-ranking demon, was the head possessor in a particularly nasty case. The afflicted young woman was regularly assaulted and manipulated by demons. The exorcism sessions were intense and full of swearing, yelling, growling, lewd gestures, and vomiting.

At the end of the most recent session, the young woman came back to herself after being in an active demonic state for almost an hour. I asked, as I typically do at the end of every session, "How are you? What happened during the session?" She said, "Baphomet is angry with you. He said that he is going to get you tonight at midnight."

This is not the first time the demons have threatened one of us exorcists. Sometimes they will tell the Exorcist *when* they will attack and at other times they leave it unknown. But our experience is that when they say they will attack the priest, they will indeed do so. It is not a bluff. However, the Evil One is not allowed to do any more than what God allows and He always provides the graces to overcome any and all demonic assaults.

"Forewarned is forearmed." A few hours before midnight, another priest exorcist kindly prayed some deliverance prayers over me. I believe this had the effect of somewhat blunting the coming attack. I then commended myself to the protection of the Blessed Virgin, sprinkled holy water around the room, and went to bed.

Around midnight, I was awakened by intense agitation and temptations. These were followed by feelings of utter darkness. Recognizing the source of these strong mental attacks, I then said three times out loud: "I offer these assaults for the liberation of the afflicted person." Instantly, the assaults lessened in intensity. Not only is this offering helpful for the afflicted person, it also impresses upon the demons, once again, that all of their efforts are self-defeating. Everything they do ultimately redounds to the glory of God and furthers God's Kingdom. The attacks did not dissipate completely until a couple of hours had passed. Then, I went back to bed and slept soundly, having once again experienced the surpassing power of Christ and his defeat of Satan.

Often possessed people are so afraid of the demons that it keeps them from doing what they need to do to get rid of them. The demons constantly threaten them. A possessed woman recently told me: "I don't go to Church and the Mass because the demons told me not to. They threaten to kill me if I do." Of course, it is precisely going to Mass and receiving the sacraments that is critical for getting rid of the demons. And a person's fear of the demons actually "feeds" them—it makes them stronger and even harder to expel.

When the demons say they do not want us to do something, this is a good indication that it is vitally important to do it. In the midst of an exorcism, I recall the demons demanded in a threatening tone to take the priest's stole off the neck of the afflicted person, which was touched to the neck of the person during the prayers. I doubled down. In response, I put two stoles on her neck and left them there for a long time. No doubt, the grace of this sacramental was being particularly efficacious against this set of demons.

Giving into fear of Satan and his minions only empowers the demons. Faith is more than simply acknowledging that God exists. It implies trusting in God and in the victory of Jesus Christ. We know that Satan and the demons are chained and can only do what God allows. And God does not allow them directly to kill or maim anyone. One proof is that if God did allow demons to kill people, every exorcist would be dead within 24 hours.

It is particularly difficult for possessed people to muster the courage to disobey the demons and trust in God. They hear and sometimes "see" the demons. And they hear the violent demonic threats and can be cowered by their intense evil. But the path to liberation requires just such a trust in God and a rejection of evil.

So, too, for us exorcists. We must surrender ourselves completely into God's hands. Nothing happens that is not allowed by God. We trust in Him. We go forward with our ministry, directly confronting Evil, confident in this knowledge and surrendering ourselves into His hands. In the midst of a difficult exorcism, when the afflicted person is frightened, I ask them to pray with me: "Jesus, I trust in you. Jesus, I trust in you."

Slimed and Attacked by Demons

IT WAS A ROUGH CASE FOR SURE, BUT MUCH PROGRESS WAS BEING MADE. Several lay team members and priests were present for each session. For this one particular session, the afflicted person's priest-spiritual director was also present, which we encourage. It was his first participation in a solemn exorcism of a possessed person.

For solemn exorcisms especially, we carefully screen who is in the room. We admit only mature Catholics who are strong in faith with a recognized calling for this ministry. Still, the first session can be a bit overwhelming, especially when there is a strong manifestation of the demonic. Nothing can really prepare you to look into the face of such evil. It can be quite unnerving.

When the lengthy session ended, the Exorcist, as always, prayed the cleansing and protection prayers. Then the team adjourned to the next room to meet and recap. The priest-spiritual director was present as well. At one point, the priest tried to speak but kept messing up his words. He said he couldn't think straight and had problems talking coherently. He was confused and added, "I can't understand why my brain is not working." The Exorcist asked him about his symptoms in more depth. Borrowing a popular movie expression, he concluded, "It sounds like you've been 'slimed.'" The Exorcist then reminded him of a movie scene when an evil presence went through a person leaving behind a slimy residue which mentally disoriented him. "Yeah," the priest said recalling the movie incident, "It kinda felt like that."

So the Exorcist did another round of cleansing prayers for him and the entire team. These "prayers for protection" and the "cleansing prayers" at the beginning and end of an exorcism session are important and largely effective.[5] But in tough cases, some demonic effects can break through. At such times, a second round of cleansing is needed. After this second cleansing round of prayers, his confusion lifted and his mind started to work normally again.

As an exorcism team, we endeavor to practice our ministry with integrity. We are obedient to all the Church teaches and to our ecclesiastical superiors. It is important for us to "stay under the umbrella" of the Church's protection. We willingly do so. Nevertheless, in particularly difficult cases, we can get "slimed" and have some passing, limited demonic symptoms.

Moreover, some team members are "burden bearers." These are folks, chosen by God and not by the individuals themselves, who participate in Christ's bearing of people's burdens. More than a spiritual sensitivity, burden bearers actually feel and experience, to some degree, the sufferings of the other. Often this means experiencing some of the demonic attacks normally visited on the afflicted person.

Jesus is THE burden bearer. In his death and resurrection, he took upon himself all of our sins and became the source of salvation. But, at times, some are called to participate in the sufferings of others and the redemption wrought in Christ. Galatians 6:2 might be applied: "Bear one another's burdens, and so you will fulfill the law of Christ."

In another case, we were trying to discern whether the person had a demonic presence or perhaps the symptoms were of a psychological origin. One of our burden bearers was present and after the session she said, "I experienced a spirit of terror, and demonic mental attacks. It was very strong." Her intervention was helpful input into the Exorcist's discernment. He decided to continue the deliverance sessions. Later sessions confirmed her experience.

When the Spirit has burden bearers take on the sufferings of others, it typically helps afflicted individuals with their sufferings. It may give them a slight respite which can be critical in a time of crisis. It also helps to discern what the underlying wounds are and may be an occasion of a unique healing grace.

In our exorcism ministry, we have such generous people and we are VERY grateful for them. Their ministry is largely hidden and should remain so. They participate in the cross of Jesus for others. It is not an easy calling.

And all of us who experience some kind of demonic attack in the wake of an exorcism consider it to be a small price for another person's liberation. We pray that our little sacrifices are an additional grace to the suffering people who come to us for help. Our hearts go out to them and we pray for their swift deliverance.

Demon Brain

IT IS BECOMING APPARENT TO ME THAT MORE THAN A FEW OF THOSE MENTALLY TORMENTED BY THEIR SINS AND FAILINGS OF THE PAST ARE ACTUALLY SUFFERING FROM DEMONIC OBSESSIONS OR, AS WE CALL IT, DEMON BRAIN. There is a natural psychological OCD (obsessive compulsive disorder) where a person obsessively ruminates about a real, or imagined, failing from the past. In the more severe cases, these ruminations, and unsuccessful attempts to rid oneself of them (compulsions), can be debilitating. Such individuals are usually best treated by a combination of CBT (Cognitive-Behavioral Therapy) and medications.

But there is sometimes, masked within the deceptive trappings of an OCD disorder, an actual attack by the Evil One. One senior exorcist estimated that 25 percent of the population is suffering from some form of demonic obsessions. I have no reason to believe that figure is exaggerated.

For example, "John" was tormented by evil and blasphemous thoughts to the point of no longer being able to function. Years of psychotherapy brought no relief. It was noteworthy that these obsessions began after his having relapsed into pornography. Confession, amending his life, and a handful of deliverance sessions all but extinguished the mental obsessions.

Similarly, "Alicia" was tormented with thoughts of self-hatred and despair, often bringing her to the brink of suicide. While psychotherapy was helpful, the mental attacks were intense and out of proportion to her psychological state. Moreover, the attacks began whenever she tried to pray or go to Mass. She, too, found considerable relief through active renunciation of the demonic thoughts and subsequent deliverance sessions.

In both cases, the mental obsessions are not completely gone, because their root is in their normal psychological weaknesses. But it became clear that Satan, being an opportunist, was exploiting their human weaknesses. He exaggerated their weaknesses to the point of complete dysfunction, despair, and suicidality. Now, Alicia and John suffer with a much-reduced, normal, human weakness. With virtuous sacramental living and prayer, the demonic ferocity of the attacks dissipated.

Demonic obsessions can be distinguished from psychological OCD ruminations by their intensity, being out of proportion to one's human state, and the ferocity of the mental attack. Also, there is usually an opening to the demonic that can be identified, especially in recent sinful practices and/or occult practices. Finally, the intensity of the mental attacks dissipates in the wake of deliverance prayers.

When discerning whether someone has a demonic problem or not, I typically ask what messages they are hearing in their heads. Over the years, I have heard the demonically possessed and oppressed/obsessed consistently relate six basic messages. Satan whispers (or yells!) these in people's heads without respite:

1. *You are a terrible person.*
2. *There is no hope for you.*
3. *God doesn't care about you.*
4. *You're mine. I will never leave.*
5. *You are going to hell.*
6. *You should kill yourself.*

There is a little bit of this mental negativism in all fallen human beings, we who are tainted by Original Sin. But when Satan is doing it directly, the message is loud, consistent, and unrelenting. I personally believe that more than a few people take their own lives being worn down after years of this mental battle. Sadly, in hell where there are no chains on Satan and his minions, the demons will torment souls with these demonic thoughts without end.

What to do in this life? I recommend people confront this on both the natural and supernatural planes. On the natural level, Satan gets a foothold in people's psyches through their human weaknesses and sins. In this case, the more damaged our psyches, the stronger this negative self-talk in our heads. Satan will exploit this weakness.

So, we should engage normal human remedies for such mental negativity. For example, a variety of cognitive-behavioral interventions can be a help. There are a plethora of these on-line. Counseling by a licensed professional, who is supportive of the faith, might also bring some healing to the roots. For more serious cases, medications for obsessive-compulsive thinking may be indicated.

But for those suffering from demon brain, i.e., Satan strongly influencing the thoughts in their heads, a regimen of deliverance prayers coupled with the holy sacraments and a prayer life are essential.

At the end of one's life, this demonic obsessive assault is sometimes no longer hidden. As one enters the final judgment, Satan, the great accuser, may accuse the soul of all its infidelities in life. He demands that it be justly consigned to hell. As St. Catherine of Siena relates in *The Dialogue*, the Lord revealed to her that: "In the moment of death...the Devil accuses them with great terror and darkness...the Devil torments him with [his] infidelity in order to bring him to despair."[6] The soul's recourse in extremity, and always, is the mercy of God. Jesus paid the price for our sins. We are saved in this life, and the next, by the love of our merciful God and the sacrifice of the Son.

Satan can only give to people what he has: hopelessness, self-hatred and despair. The final antidote to Satan's messages and the resulting demon brain is the Good News of Jesus. This supernatural battle can only be finally resolved on the supernatural plane. Once we know deeply in our hearts that God loves us personally, and that we are saved by the blood of the Lamb, then our minds can fully be at peace.

Seven Signs of Satan's Hidden Presence

SATAN'S FIRST AND BEST TACTIC IS TO HIDE. He is most effective when he makes us believe that his awful and sickening influence comes from inside us. He wants us to think that his anger, torment, and hatred are part of who we are and to make us feel that we are beyond love and redemption. As noted in a previous chapter, he wants us to believe that the onslaught of negative mental self-messages, i.e. demon brain, comes from ourselves.

Based on our experience with those who suffer demonic afflictions, we might identify seven common signs of the Evil One's hidden presence. They are:

- *lethargy & fatigue*
- *nausea and headaches*
- *awful, sick feeling in the entire body*
- *exaggerated anger and bursts of rage*
- *evil spirit of division, distrust and conflict*
- *negative mental self-messages (i.e. demon brain)*
- *exaggerated sexual temptations & intrusive blasphemous thoughts*

These seven symptoms often have natural causes. For example, most headaches and nausea have a bio-psychological cause. But when the Evil One is present, it is very common that people will have headaches, stomachaches, nausea, and a general sick feeling. This is also common with spiritual sensitives as we shall later discuss. The presence of demons will typically be felt by sensitives with these aforementioned physical symptoms, which is why training and direction is important; it can help sensitives understand what is happening to them and guide their efforts.

Similarly, during our online deliverance sessions, more than a few comment that after the prayers start, they are overcome with feelings of lethargy and fatigue. However, when I explicitly cast out demons of fatigue and lethargy, their symptoms often dissipate. Similarly, when the demonically afflicted come to an exorcism session, it is not uncommon that they will be abnormally tired and lethargic. This is a sign that the demons are starting to manifest in them.

And, of course, a hallmark of the presence of evil is a spirit of distrust, division and conflict. I recall one religious telling me that their community was gathering for their biannual chapter meeting. An unexpected intense and inexplicable conflict erupted and threatened the entire process. The quick-thinking superior suspected a demonic cause. He stopped the meeting and had everyone pray to cast out any evil spirits present and to promote the good Spirit of unity. When they resumed the chapter, everything went well and a spirit of unity and grace reigned.

All of these symptoms can, and typically do, have underlying normal human roots. But Satan is an opportunist and exploits our natural human weaknesses and exaggerates them, which makes them even more difficult to spot. For example, a person with a penchant for sexual temptations will be bombarded by the Evil One with intense sexual images and impulses, not realizing that Satan is fueling the person's normal weakness into a raging fire.

What to do? Whenever these ugly symptoms surface, people should first look for a natural cause and deal with it on the human level. However, if the evil symptoms come on unexpectedly, suddenly and fiercely, then people might suspect them as coming from the Evil One and reject them. They might use the three R's: "I reject them; I rebuke them; I renounce them, and in Jesus' holy name I cast them out."

What is usually most effective is a combination of natural healing and deliverance prayers. The deliverance prayers can cast out the exaggerated demonic interference and natural healing methods can be important in healing any underlying weaknesses which give the demons an opening. Healing inner wounds, fears, unforgiveness and angers are particularly important. We often ask people to see a Catholic psychotherapist to address these inner wounds so the demons don't keep coming back.

As long as Satan's presence is hidden and unrecognized, he is more able to manipulate his victims. Once his presence is unmasked, it is much easier to deal with his ugly presence and demonic symptoms in a direct and effective way. When Satan is unmasked and can no longer hide, he is well on the way to being defeated and cast out.

Ghosts or Demons?

EXORCISTS OFTEN GET ASKED ABOUT "GHOSTS" AND/ OR "STUCK SOULS" THAT HAUNT PLACES. These are human souls who are thought to inhabit places after their deaths, perhaps due to some unfinished business that needs to be resolved before their final rest. What does the Church have to say?

Every exorcist knows how critical it is that he operates completely obedient to the teachings of the Church. Whenever he strays from such, it is an opening to the demonic which definitely will be exploited by the Evil One. Moreover, obedience exercised by the afflicted, the Exorcist and Team aids in the expulsion of the demons. Demons hate obedience. Not long ago, I was in the midst of a session and prayed to the Blessed Virgin Mary to give the afflicted person a "double grace of obedience" and the demons' negative reaction was strong. They were repulsed by it.

The Catholic Catechism summarizes the Church teaching on the disposition of departed souls: "Each man receives his eternal retribution in his immortal soul at the very moment of his death, in a particular judgment" (CCC, 1022). The soul is immediately committed to heaven, hell or to a time of purgation before heaven. There are no other choices and there is no delay in this particular judgment. Thus, there are no souls who have not received judgment and thus no "stuck souls" per se.

Does this mean that deceased souls cannot visit us on earth? St. Thomas Aquinas weighed in saying:

"According to the disposition of Divine providence separated souls sometimes come forth from their abode and appear to men" (ST, suppl, Q. 69, A.3). He wrote that souls in heaven can wondrously visit us as a special grace. Many blessed persons on earth have been granted the grace of the visit of a saint from heaven. Souls in hell can, by a specific act of God, be allowed to visit the living for "man's instruction and intimidation" so that we, too, might not end up in such an awful place. And souls in purgatory can appear to the living "in order to seek our suffrages" to aid in their final liberation into heaven.

Many a saint has been visited by a soul in purgatory and asked for the saint's intercession to be released more quickly from its torment. The lives of the saints are replete with such experiences. For example, Padre Pio claimed, "As many souls of the dead come up this road [to the monastery] as that of the souls of the living."[7] The prayers of this holy monk released many of the living and the dead from evil.

However, when encountering spirits in a place, it is safest to first assume that it is an evil spirit and to have it exorcized. Demons often try to disguise themselves as good spirits in order to develop an unholy relationship with its victims. One sign of a demonic presence is their negative, harmful effects; they are vicious and destructive. However, it is generally thought that human souls in purgatory, allowed to request our assistance, are not harmful and merely want to get our attention for prayer and suffrages. If the spirit present seems to be benign and not vengeful or harmful, and there are solid reasons to believe that it is a soul doing its purgation, then prayers and Masses might be offered for its repose.

A word of caution. More than a few have believed that they were dealing with benign human souls when, in fact, they were engaged with demons. Also, it is very unwise to engage in any sort of communication with such spirits, evil or benign. I know a man who became possessed after an unholy interest and visits to haunted houses and ghost hunting. His unholy interest and personal sins made him vulnerable, and his frequenting these "haunted" locations actually put him in regular contact with the demonic. The currently popular "ghost hunting" craze is a spiritually dangerous idea. I suspect that many are spiritually unprotected individuals, with possible personal openings to the demonic, who are entering the realm of the dark world for unholy reasons. This is a recipe for disaster.

Also, beware of thinking one has a special charism to help "stuck souls." This could easily be the sin of spiritual pride. There are some, even priests, who believe they have a special gift to be in touch with "stuck souls" and to help them to transition fully to the next life. I wonder with whom they are really communicating. Rather, we should simply offer prayers and Masses for the deceased souls who need them, as all the pious should do.

There is an unholy interest and fascination today with the paranormal and with fringe "supernatural" experiences. I stick with what the Church has to offer: the lives of canonized saints (which are often filled with miraculous events), approved apparitions of the BVM, and, of course, the central focus on the truly miraculous and saving life of Jesus Christ. All these safely lead us to God, where our focus should be.

Financial Curses

A MAN'S CRY FOR HELP CAUGHT MY EYE. He wrote to me:

"I own my own business. Large amounts of money come through but I can never keep any of it. If it looks like I will have a little profit from a job, something unexpected will ALWAYS pop up and take it, like a vehicle breaking down, even though there was absolutely nothing wrong with it before. Recently a customer wanted to pay their final payment with a credit card. I have three different credit card systems, each under different companies, but the day I went to collect the payment none of them would work... The attack I am undergoing feels more like a curse or a spell...I must add that I do not feel that God has failed me, because whatever this is never seems to win completely. I have managed to keep my head just above water."

These were just a few of his examples of this man's strangely-failed finances. The man had many more!

A young family came to me with a similar story. The father had a good job with the government and was a fiscally responsible adult. But the family was constantly broke due to a bizarre, never-ending series of financial setbacks. It was more than a case of bad luck. Like the above businessman, this man felt that he was financially cursed.

A third person beset with similar inexplicable financial setbacks started to find small coins around his house (dimes and pennies) and sometimes in his pocket with no awareness of how they got there. The man said, "About once a week I find a dime in my left pocket. We have been struggling financially. Barely making enough to eat." It felt to him and his wife that demons were taunting them. It is true that some people are not good with money and overspend. They might benefit from help in financial management. But these strange cases are a bit "over the top" and one suspects some evil is directly involved.

I am running into more and more cases of what appears to be a financial curse. The stories are similar. They are fiscally responsible people. They relate a long series of unforeseen financial setbacks. The financial reversals come out of nowhere and never seem to end. In the beginning, they thought it was just a bad run of luck. But eventually they realize that something evil is afoot. They feel cursed. Some can actually trace the beginning of their financial misfortunes to a specific individual who cursed them. Others recall a family history of the occult or other demonic portals. And like a case of possession, there are limits on what God allows the Evil One to do to them. They hover on the brink of financial disaster and destitution, but never seem to go over the line.

The first step in overcoming a financial curse is, of course, to live in a state of grace. For Catholics, this includes frequent confession, Mass and Eucharist plus avoiding serious sin.

Second, one needs to close any possible portals to the demonic. In one case, a financially cursed individual had a strong family history of freemasonry. It is not surprising that someone's involvement in freemasonry would lead to financial curses, since many join in hopes of financial gain and social success. The afflicted individual was led through the ritual of renouncing freemasonic curses.

Another couple with financial problems had been cursed by an angry grandparent who did not approve of their marriage. She admitted going to a witch to invoke her black magic and cursed them saying, "You will have nothing." The antidote for them included breaking any unholy connection with the grandparent, the witch, and lifting all the curses.

Because these curses came through the evil and sins of someone in one's blood line, they can take time to expunge. Consistent prayer, deliverance, holy living and trusting in Jesus are necessary. But it is not always "one and done." Ultimately, liberation is in the Lord's time, and there may be an extended period of financial distress. When we trust in the Lord during times of trial, there is much purification and sanctification that occurs.

At the end of this book is a prayer to assist in counteracting a financial curse. It recognizes that individuals have natural law rights over their own bodies and their finances and possessions. Thus, they can command the demons to depart from themselves and they can lift any curses against themselves. Such a prayer can be said daily. If needed, a priest can ratify the prayer and he can invoke the Church's authority in lifting the curse and casting out any related demons. A powerful help to the process of liberation is consecrating one's life and goods to the Blessed Virgin Mary. This can be formally done in the St. Louis de Montfort consecration.[8]

Satan's Plan and the Demonic Inversion

SATAN HAS A PLAN. He is cunning and more intelligent than we can imagine. He has a plan and all of his actions are in service of that plan. Demons don't do "random," even if their actions initially seem to be without reason. Their actions conform to the Satanic plan, which ultimately is self-defeating, as evil must be and is.

I recall one moment that the demons were lamenting what a particular Catholic mystic and victim soul was doing. Through her, much good was being done in a specific area, which the demons were seeking to control. At one point the demons confessed the truth, obviously under God's command since they normally do not tell the truth. They admitted: "She is destroying our plans!" Yes, Satan has an evil plan which, of its nature, cannot succeed.

Essentially his plan is to destroy God's kingdom. In service of that plan, he tries to destroy everything and everyone. He is in a rage against God and anything God has created. He is especially enraged about God becoming flesh in Jesus and thus attempts to destroy anything connected to Jesus, including every human person. He desires to drag every soul created in God's image into his reign in hell.

I find it incredible these days that more than a few people are trying to "redeem" Satan's image. Some proclaim: "Satan loves you" or others claim that Satan is for equality and justice for all, especially the marginalized. Others claim he is a great promoter of humanity and a great humanist. Some, including prominent Churchmen, simply say he does not exist.

These are part of Satan's tactics: the *demonic inversion*. He proposes lies in place of truth; he convinces people that the truth is a lie. He suggests that what is evil is good and what is good is evil. Satan's kingdom takes the truth and goodness and turns it on its head. For a rational Christian, listening to members of Satanic cults can be baffling. How can they believe such lies and drivel about Satan? It helps to understand that cult members have probably been traveling a long dark road for many years and their minds are filled with demonic darkness and lies. Their minds are filled with Satan's inversion of the truth.

We see this demonic inversion not only in the thinking of the followers of Satan, but we, frighteningly, see it increasingly cropping up everywhere in today's society. For example, a family television channel has decided to air a program in which a young 18-year-old woman falls in love with and has a sexual encounter with Satan. She becomes pregnant. The show is being advertised as a "coming of age" event for this young woman. I cannot think of anything more evil than giving one's self to Satan in a sexual encounter![9] On the other hand, it has become forbidden in some circumstances and places to display Christian symbols. Christian prayers are forbidden in many public events. So, it is forbidden in our society to pray to God but one can have sex with Satan? This is most certainly a Satanic inversion!

This Satanic inversion infects the minds of the possessed. As noted previously, a huge difficulty in the early stages of a case of strong possession is dealing with these inversions or, what we earlier called: "demon brain." The farther one goes into the clutches of Satan and his dark kingdom, the more one begins to think like demons. They believe Satan's inversion of the truth. This is part of Satan's plan: to make everyone and everything in his own image, as a mockery of God's kingdom.

It is part of his plan of destruction. In the clutches of Satan, there is a darkness and heaviness that comes over the person's mind and heart. I find this especially true of those who practice witchcraft, magic and other forms of divination. For example, a young man in his 30's came in for help. He had been practicing witchcraft for a number of years and started his own coven. As he sat in front of me, there was a strong sense of darkness and heaviness about him. And I told him so. He admitted it and knew that his practice of witchcraft was leading him down a dark path. His mind was filled with increasingly dark thoughts. Sadly he did not pursue an exorcism because he apparently did not want to give up the feeling of power that witchcraft gave him, despite its increasingly destructive hold on him.

This demon brain and its concomitant increasing darkness in the mind makes an exorcism difficult, especially in the early stages. In the beginning, possessed peoples' minds are filled with all sorts of demonic lies which they have a hard time disbelieving. They are often convinced they are beyond hope and that they belong to Satan. They do not believe that God cares about them or could forgive their sins. They are often aware of Satan's considerable power, but have no sense of God's surpassing, infinite power. They typically are distrusting, full of fear and despair, and many times flooded with anger. In short, their minds are filled with demonic attributes—demon brain. As an exorcist, I have to go slowly with the possessed and exercise much patience.

As one senior exorcist told me: "An exorcism is the process of pouring the truth down the demon's throat." They cannot stand the truth. They especially cannot stand the ultimate Truth: Jesus. They are inveterate liars and evil spawns of the Father of Lies. Exorcism prayers simply tell Satan the truth about who he really is and who God is. Also, it tells him about the coming final judgment, of which he is rightly terrified.

One of the graces of the ministry of exorcism is that our exorcists, team members, and the possessed daily experience the truths of the faith. One possessed woman, who had a strong demonic possession including the presence of high-ranking demons, said to me: "I have met Satan and he is vicious!" She knows, by personal experience, the truth of who Satan is.

One of the ways we discern the presence of Satan and his minions is by "the look."[10] In the midst of an exorcism, the demons typically manifest their presence, especially on the face of the energumen (possessed person). The demons come forward and the person's personality recedes into the background. Sometimes, the person is unconscious, especially in stronger cases of possession. In weaker cases of possession, the person may retain consciousness but the person is looking in from the background while the demons take over. When the demons do come forward, their presence is unmistakable: the look on their face is complete evil.

Looking into the face of this evil, there is no doubt about Satan's intentions. He will torture and destroy you if he can. The fact that he cannot is a strong affirmation of the presence of God and his triumph over Satan. Satan is a chained beast. But like all chained beasts, do not get too close. He is deadly. If you open yourself to Satan and put yourself into his grasp, he will certainly, bit by bit, destroy you. This is Satan's plan.

More on the Demonic Inversion

ONE OF THE MOST SIGNIFICANT EXAMPLES OF SATAN'S MOCKERY OF GOD THROUGH AN INVERSION OF THE SACRED IS THE *black mass*. It is interesting that they steal a consecrated host from a Catholic Church and desecrate it during their "mass." Satan is unwittingly witnessing to the sanctity of the true Mass, the real spiritual power of the Catholic priesthood and Church, and the true presence of Christ in the Eucharist.

One exorcist reported that, in the midst of an exorcism, the demons let out an exasperated exclamation: "All those Masses!" Clearly, Satan's kingdom is being pummeled by the many Catholic Masses daily said throughout the world.

Another demonic inversion occurs on the eve of major holy days such as "All Hallows Eve," that is, *Halloween*. It is the eve of a wonderful holy day of the Feast of All Saints. On this date, the Church recognizes and celebrates the sanctity of all those countless numbers of souls who are in heaven, although not officially canonized. We especially celebrate our loved ones who have gone before us and have entered the Kingdom. We are grateful for them. We rely on their prayers and intercession.

It is well known in our deliverance circles that Satan and his minions are especially active on Halloween. As Feast of All Saints gets closer, we get ready for a demonic onslaught on Halloween. Witches are cursing us. The possessed often experience especially strong demonic attacks that evening. Our exorcists and staff are the targets of demonic attacks as well. This last Halloween was ugly and required the lifting of curses and some additional cleansing prayers.

Some Halloween traditions actually carry over vestiges of this spiritual warfare. For example, carved pumpkins with scary faces likely originated from a recognition that demons are especially powerful on Halloween. Pumpkins or large gourds with scary faces were thought to be a kind of talisman to scare away these evil spirits. Gargoyles on ancient cathedrals in Europe had a similar function. It seems odd to see such demonic looking images on a Catholic cathedral. However, many ascribe a similar kind of apotropaic function, i.e., warding off demons. Of course, we Christians do not believe in or use talismans such as a rabbit's foot, nazars to ward off the evil eye, or any kind of good luck charm. The appropriate accoutrements for a Catholic include such items as a crucifix, a medal of a saint, rosary beads or a brown scapular. These are not pagan talismans but rather sacramentals that invoke the saving power of Christ.

There are many other examples of demonic inversions. One need only look at the literature from a Satanic cult to recognize perversions of the sacred at every turn. Statues of Baphomet, a major demon, have been erected or attempted to be placed in public areas. On the other hand, statues of saints and the Virgin Mary are regularly being desecrated and destroyed in record numbers around the United States. Some elementary schools have allowed after school Satanic clubs, while traditional Christian prayers are disallowed in schools.

Many forms of magic are perversions of Catholic prayers and liturgies. The term "hocus pocus" is actually derived from the Latin words of consecration at the Mass: *Hoc est enim corpus meum* (this is my body).

Satan's mockery of all that belongs to God is his own witness, albeit unintentional, to the Sacred and its supreme importance. It was Lucifer's intention to become like God, and thus imitate all things holy. Evil is an imitation of the good but with a flaw, a defect. It might initially look or model that which is good, but, in the end, it only leads to destruction and death.

Attacked by Witches

I HAVE FELT IT PARTICULARLY IMPORTANT TO WARN PEO-
PLE ABOUT WITCHCRAFT. Many witches don't believe in
Satan. Many practitioners of "magick" believe they are
tapping into some unique spiritual energy. One witch
claimed to be using the ancient power of the Druids; another claimed to be using the "feminine energy of the
Universe." Another witch publicly claimed that she is
invoking the goddess Hecate. Interestingly enough, in
one of our exorcism cases, one of the demons present
identified itself as Hecate.

One witch actually admitted she was using demons,
but she foolishly added, "I can control the demons." I
often say that there are no such abstract spiritual energies in the universe that these New Agers often invoke.
If they are not invoking the power of the true God, then
the only other spiritual force in the universe comes from
the dark world. They are unwitting minions of Satan
and are actually being used by him.

Witches have taken my videos and stitched them
into their online posts. They have made me a target of
their curses. A senior exorcist said, with insight from a
spiritually sensitive person, that my name is prominent
on the blackboard in hell. I am on Satan's short list for
harassment and destruction, which I suspect is true of
every faithful exorcist. We trust in God's protection.

Now, the witches have added me to their list. I know
that some people, including priests, are afraid to confront evil forces. They do not want to rile Satan or get

his attention. They are afraid of being cursed or being attacked by demons. But if we have not upset the dark world even a little, have we truly preached the Gospel? Faith is more than simply believing that God exists. It means trusting in Him and his supreme power and love, and actively doing His will.

I should not and do not intentionally try to rile anyone. It would be an act of hubris to think that I should directly confront Satan or his minions. St. Gemma Galgani, mystic and saint, used to refer to herself as "poor Gemma." I feel like "poor Steve." Who am I?

Rather, I hide behind Jesus. I let him speak through me as best I can. I let him cast out demons. I let his Word speak to the world. It is the humility of the Blessed Virgin Mary which confounds Satan. It is the humility of Jesus on the cross which destroyed Satan's kingdom of arrogance. I must be little and small. Nevertheless, here I am: my name in bold letters in hell and a target on my back for demons and witches.

A few nights ago, I was awakened abruptly. I was being attacked by demons. It felt like a dozen of them had jumped me and were pummeling me with their fists. In an instance, I had a spiritual vision from the Lord. I saw the witches' coven that was cursing me. There were about 5 to 8 of them; all white middle-aged women. I saw one woman who appeared to be their leader: white hair, anglo, and a little plump.

I instantly started to pray an exorcism prayer and within a couple of minutes, the demons departed. Then I felt the "slime" of their curses that was still on me. Several times I prayed: "May the blood of Jesus wash over me and cleanse me." After a few times, I was clean. I was tired from the activities of the day and felt fast asleep.

What does this tell you? First, witches' curses are real. Some have criticized me for saying witches have power. However, it is my clear and repeated experience that real witches (not the dabblers) do command spiritual power. But it is only a power of darkness; it is the power of demons. What can a witch do? They can do anything a demon can do because all of their powers come from demons. This makes witches angry when I say it, but I speak the truth.

Second, their power is nothing compared to Jesus. A group of them gave it their best shot and within a few moments, one solitary priest using the power of Christ nullified their curses and cast out all their little demons. The next morning I prayed the "Prayer Against Trafficking Witches" which is found at the end of this book and on our app and website. These trafficking or traveling witches projected their evil power against me. This prayer does not pray for their destruction but rather it beseeches God for their conversion. They are deep into the dark world and cannot see or understand the Truth. It is a joy to recognize that a number of high-ranking witches have indeed been converted to Christ, according to their own testimony. Thanks be to God!

The prayer also attempts to "de-fang" these witches so they cannot harm anyone else. It attempts to take away their dark powers. Of course, whether the prayer is effective depends upon what God will permit. I prayed that He would permit this prayer to take away their evil spiritual powers. I do not know if it worked. But I trust in Him.

I truly have no hard feelings against these witches. I prayed a little prayer to forgive them, and I meant it.

They are being deceived and on the road to destruction. They must realize that their curses were quickly rendered ineffective by Jesus. Should that not tell them something? Moreover, the ones who are first and most cursed by their spells are themselves.

Some time ago I had an encounter with some demons that I often cite. While I am careful not to overstep safe boundaries as an exorcist, I sometimes grill them during a session to admit the Truth of who and what they have become, which is itself exorcistic and found in the Rite of Exorcism. I said to them: "In the holy name of Jesus, I command you to tell me the truth. Who is Lord? Satan or Jesus? Tell the truth!" They were loathe to respond but they were forced to do so. With a low voice and a snarl they said, "Jesus."

The demons know that Jesus is Lord. Satan has lost and his kingdom has been smashed. I pray these witches learn the Truth as well before it is too late for them. They still have time to turn from the darkness. But the fallen angels are lost forever.

Powerful Intercessors in Heaven

ONE OF OUR EXORCISTS BEGAN TO PRAY OVER A POSSESSED WOMAN. At the very beginning of the session, the demons spontaneously shouted, "Charbel, you stay away from me!" But the team had not yet been invoking the saints, or St. Charbel by name, so they were surprised he showed up in anticipation. They were also surprised the demons admitted it. Moments later, as the Litany of the Saints ensued, the demons shouted again and again after the names of several saints were mentioned: "Not that name! Not that name!" This demonic reaction was unusual. Clearly something was up.

An astute exorcist typically discerns what is working in a session and adjusts the prayers accordingly. In this case, the Exorcist was initially skeptical, as he should be, and careful not to be deceived by the demons. But as the session continued, it was becoming apparent that these and many other saints were indeed coming to help. Their holiness and intercession were visibly torturing the demons.

Normally, the Litany of the Saints is part of the opening prayers of every exorcism. Then the Exorcist may move quickly into what he might think to be "more important" prayers. However, in this case, the Exorcist adjusted his normal routine and stayed with the Litany of the Saints for almost two hours, making it the bulk of the session.

Also, he had dozens of first-class relics of the saints at his fingertips, which are tiny fragments of the body of a saint housed in a theca or other sacred reliquary. As the Exorcist prayed each name, he laid the corresponding relic of the saint on the afflicted person's forehead. With each relic and invocation of a saint, the demons howled in agony.

The three consecutive days of intensive exorcism sessions over the one energumen were focused on and filled with hours of invoking the saints. Again and again, the demons shouted, "Not that name! Not that name!" as he invoked St. Patrick, St. Rose of Lima, St. Maximillian Kolbe, the 12 Apostles, St. Margaret Mary Alacoque, Blessed Michael McGivney, St. Lawrence, Blessed Conchita, St. Teresa and the Carmelite saints, St. Catherine of Alexandria, St. John Eudes, and more.

On day two, the demons began to manifest their leaving. The afflicted woman started coughing up a white frothy foam. The demonic screaming reached a crescendo followed by a kind of demonic "explosion." Then she came back to herself. Again and again, as each set of demons left, there was coughing up of foam, a crescendo and explosion, followed by a moment of calm with the person returning to her conscious self.

Finally, at the end of day three, the Exorcist invoked the special intercession of the Virgin Mary. This time, after the demonic explosion, a peace came over the woman and filled the entire room. She came back to herself and said, "It's over." She said that a great weight had been lifted and the demons were gone. Initial subsequent discernment confirmed that the demonic possession had ended.

Each possession and each path to liberation is always somewhat unique. In this case, the Exorcist believes that the Lord was teaching him and the Team the importance of the communion of the saints and their powerful intercession. Moreover, he said, "It taught me that every part of the Rite is exorcistic, not just the imprecatory prayers that command the demons to leave." Now the exorcist does not fail to value the prayers which invoke the powerful intercession of the saints. Nor should we.

But the story does not end here. Demons have committed themselves to an eternity of revenge. No doubt, they were enraged to be cast out by the saints. A few days later, they had their revenge. Shortly thereafter another of our exorcists, who is also the pastor of a parish, displayed a handful of relics of the saints for veneration in his church. For many years without incident, he has followed this practice in the month of November, the month when we venerate All Saints. This year, however, the relics were stolen.

The security cameras showed that a woman in a dark coat sat in front of the relics for some time. Then as she approached the relics, the security camera tape went inexplicably blank for five and one-half minutes. The tape subsequently showed that the reliquaries in which the relics were housed were opened and the relics (the thecas) were stolen while the reliquaries themselves were not.

One might first presume that it was a case of a simple robbery. But the reliquaries were not stolen and they most likely would be the object of a robbery. Who would steal a little piece of the bone or a drop of dried blood of a saint and leave behind a somewhat ornate gold-colored reliquary? Moreover, the five security cameras went blank precisely as she was apparently stealing them.

While we do not want to jump to conclusions, it seems more than likely that this was an intentional act to steal the sacred remains of the saints, and not a simple robbery. Also, the "malfunction" of the security camera at precisely the time of the robbery suggests that demons were directly involved in the act. It is highly unlikely the woman could have pulled off such a technical feat, but it would be a simple task for demons. And if demons were involved, then this woman was likely acting at the behest of Satan. She is likely a minion of the Evil One.

Our response? We pray for the conversion and salvation of her soul. We also pray that these holy objects will be returned. This retaliation of the Evil One against the saints only reaffirms our conviction of the importance of the saints in the battle against evil. For our ministry going forward, the Litany of the Saints and their relics will hold a place of great importance.

Satan's Minions

"A" WAS POSSESSED. It was bad enough that she had almost 900 demons, as admitted by the demons themselves. But she also had Satan's minions coming after her. In one instance, while A was sitting in the pews waiting for the Sunday Mass to begin, a middle-aged woman came in and sat behind her. The woman whispered to A that it was futile to resist and she should give up. And then she left, before the Mass began.

Eerie. She had never met this older woman before nor was the woman a member of the parish. There is no earthly reason why this woman would know that she was possessed, actively resisting the demons, and undergoing an exorcism. And it is certainly eerie that she would side with Satan and tell the afflicted person to give in to the Evil One. This woman was clearly one of Satan's minions.

In the last few years, we have had numerous instances of human beings who are minions of Satan. They have occult (hidden) knowledge of Satan's work and those souls who are targeted by the Evil One. They are sent to harass and tempt these afflicted souls.

Similarly, one of our exorcists was in his parish church. A deranged young man came up and shouted: "My Master is not happy with what you are doing!" There were inexplicable disturbances with the power to his Church and the PA system. The priest-exorcist was being harassed by the Evil One and this young man was acting as a minion of Satan.

Similarly, "K" was possessed and she, too, was being harassed by Satan's minions. For example, she had been clean from a cocaine addiction for quite some time, which is an important part of her ultimate liberation. Then a young woman showed up at her place of work and suggested that they take some cocaine. When K refused, the woman stuffed a bag of cocaine in her pocket.

A coincidence? I think not. The tempting woman had a tattoo on her neck of a serpent which stretched up to her ear. Reminiscent of Eve and the Garden of Eden, it looked as if the serpent was speaking into her ear. This is a tattoo which symbolizes the reality that Satan is speaking directly into her ear, one of his minions, and she is following him.

Moreover, in the area where K lives, there are some Satanic cults. Cult members have been showing up at her apartment and harassing her, although they never met her previously and she does not know them. But they know she is a special target of Satan, and they know where she lives. They were sent by the Evil One to harass and tempt her. At one point, they tried unsuccessfully to lure her into sex trafficking.

I am always surprised when I encounter people who willingly give themselves over to Satan's service. It is one thing to struggle with temptation and to fall into his grasp through sin. It's another thing to willingly choose to follow him. Satan's minions are sometimes given hidden knowledge of their targets provided by Satan, and they use it to harass and manipulate them. It is clear that their actions are ultimately being directed by high-ranking demons, whose tattoos and images are sometimes displayed prominently on their bodies and in their dwellings.

One of the Satanic cult members, who was eventually arrested on other charges, claimed to be receiving "sexual favors" from a fallen prostitute in hell, which was actually a demon. Actually, this is not impossible. While demons do not have bodies and cannot have physical sex with people, they can manipulate people's minds and sexually stimulate them.

We have encountered witches who likewise have occult knowledge, levy curses, and torment people. They, too, are in league with Satan. They receive their hidden knowledge from demons who direct the witches' actions, and make their curses potent.

In each of these cases, Satan has specific targets in mind. He directs his minions to carry out his will and he empowers their evil actions by the help of lesser demons. So far, each of these efforts by those in Satan's service has proved futile. The targeted individuals turned successfully to the true God for help. Satan tempted and harassed, but Jesus saved.

But what of Satan's servants? Will the King of Hell be grateful and reward them? Satan is a complete narcissist. He only does what serves him; there is no gratitude in him. He is also a sadist, and he derives pleasure from dominating, possessing and tormenting. Those who serve him on this earth may be promised great rewards but, in the end, all he can offer is pain, torment, and despair. He has nothing else to give.

Personally, I am dismayed to encounter people who willingly subject themselves to the Prince of Darkness. How could they be so blind? For those who serve Satan, despite promises to the contrary, it will never end well.

Spiritual Sensitives

A PRIEST CAME UP TO ME AND, LOOKING A LITTLE NER-VOUS, SAID, "WHEN I AM WITH PEOPLE WHO ARE INTO THE OCCULT, I CAN FEEL AN EVIL PRESENCE. In bad places, I sense the presence of demons. It's a sickening feeling, especially in my stomach and head. What is wrong with me? Am I possessed?" I asked, "How long have you had these sensations?" The priest responded, "Ever since childhood, but they are clearer and stronger now."

More than a few people have told me that they have similar spiritual experiences and they wonder if they need an exorcism. They are often quite worried and frightened. They think, "What is wrong with me that I sense the presence of evil and demons?"

We have found that a sensitivity to spiritual realities, especially the presence of evil and demons, can come from four possible sources:

1. It can be a natural charism which the person can use for good or ill. While some exorcists do not believe it can be a "natural" charism, some of us do believe it. Before the Fall of Adam and Eve, humans were thought to enjoy a natural gifted communion with the angelic world. But with the Fall, most of this has left. Young children sometimes display such an angelic awareness but lose it when they are older. What is critical for those who have a "natural

charism," is to use this for God's glory and further-
ing his Kingdom, and not for one's own self-ag-
grandizement or worse yet, in service of divination
and Satan's kingdom.

2. A spiritual sensitivity can be the result of a special
   Divine gift. Some people are acutely aware of the
   presence of demons, and sometimes angels, because
   God has given them a special grace to do so. They
   are expected to use this gift to help others. They can
   be a wonderful help in the deliverance ministry. An
   exorcism team typically has some sensitives to assist
   particularly in discernment.

3. A spiritual sensitivity can be the result of a demonic
   presence in the person's life. Being under the influence of demons can open an occult third eye and it
   makes people conscious of the preternatural world.
   Demonically afflicted people are aware of demons
   through the melding of the demonic and their own
   human consciousness. If a person comes from a
   long line of witches or occult practitioners, it would
   be likely for this sensitivity to come from the dark
   world. Or the person may be deceived by demons
   into thinking that demonic insinuations into the person's mind are from God.

4. For more than a few, it can be simply a product of
   their over-active imagination. They often describe
   fanciful perceptions which are not typical of the angelic world. Their "gift" may actually be the result
   of a kind of spiritual narcissism and pride. There are
   more than a few such individuals who claim such

gifts and offer themselves to exorcists as spiritual guides for their ministries. It is important to recognize these false mystics and not let them mislead the Church's ministry. For every true sensitive, there are many more who are misled.

I had a chat with the above-mentioned priest and it did not seem that he had a demonic presence acting in him. Moreover, he was living a virtuous life and was a solid priest. So I said to him, "While we have chatted only a short while, my impression is that you may have a graced spiritual sensitivity, which is a good thing. If you can find a knowledgeable spiritual director to assist you, this sensitivity of yours may be developed and assist you in your priestly ministry." He was relieved and went away in peace.

It is speculated that before the Fall of Adam and Eve, humans naturally conversed with angels and had access to the preternatural world. But when sin entered, our spiritual senses became darkened. Apparently some people retain a residual of this original grace. They are aware of angelic presences, especially demonic spirits. They feel spiritual things and sense them, although they typically remain silent for fear of others, or they themselves, will think they are crazy.

Those who work in the deliverance ministry and do exorcisms on a regular basis are daily interacting with the preternatural world. I have seen some of these individuals, laity and priests, eventually develop their innate spiritual giftedness in this regard. As time goes on in this ministry, they become more sensitive to the spirits around them.

Such gifts are helpful in our ministry. When someone comes in for an initial assessment, we typically will have at least one spiritual sensitive in the room. We use a variety of ways to discern the presence of evil spirits, including the feedback of the sensitives. In order to make a firm discernment, we look for a confluence of several indicators pointing to the same conclusion. We would not use the discernment of a sensitive alone or as primary.

As the Scriptures advise us: "Beloved, do not trust every spirit but test the spirits to see whether they belong to God, because many false prophets have gone out into the world" (1Jn 4:1). Even the most solid of spiritual sensitives can be mistaken so we take their input as one indicator but not the only indicator.

Moreover, there are many who claim to have special spiritual gifts but are mistaken. They are either mentally unstable or have an overactive imagination. Some are actually being deceived by the Evil One. Great caution is needed. I have seen more than one exorcist led down the wrong path by a person with a false charism.

But this does not warrant dismissing the reality of spiritual sensitivity altogether. There is a reality here which needs discernment and proper development. We have found such gifted people to be a grace for our ministry.

Burden Bearers

CLOSELY CONNECTED TO "SPIRITUAL SENSITIVES" ARE "BURDEN BEARERS." In addition to being sensitives, as noted earlier, some actually carry a bit of the spiritual burden of others. Typically, the night before an exorcism, or even during the exorcism itself, a burden bearer will experience some of the demonic torment of the afflicted person.

For example, a "burden bearer" might suddenly be overwhelmed with feelings of despair the night before an exorcism session. This demonic attack will come on suddenly and may last for quite a while. Then it dissipates as suddenly as it appeared. Its rapid appearance and disappearance, plus it being uncharacteristic of the burden bearer's own life, will help to identify it as a special spiritual experience. It might be related to the spiritual issues of the person who will be prayed over the next day.

The next day the burden bearer will quietly notify the Exorcist of the spiritual experience. This information can be diagnostic and help the Exorcist know what kind of demonic attacks and thus what kinds of demons the afflicted person is experiencing. Moreover, as a burden bearer, the gifted person is assisting the eventual liberation of the afflicted individual. As the burden bearer is assaulted by the person's demons, it lifts a bit of the burden from the afflicted person and the burden bearer's sacrifice is a grace in the process of liberation.

In a recent case, one of our burden bearers was a member of the Team for an afflicted person who was tormented by demons of despair, self-hatred and suicidality. What the demonically afflicted person experiences was not a normal depressed mood of the psychologically distressed. Rather, it had all the signs of being demonic. It was a demonic obsession that came over the person rapidly and the person even zoned out while the demons took over. After two days or so of being suicidal and hopeless, the mood immediately lifted and the person was back to normal. Many times, the afflicted person could not even remember what happened during those days. The night before these exorcism sessions, the burden bearer was assaulted by these demons of hopelessness and despair. It was a strong experience which came on rather suddenly, lasted about an hour or two, and then left. These experiences helped to confirm that demons were afflicting the suffering person and their type.

The next day, right before the exorcism, the burden bearer mentioned this to the Exorcist who then decided to focus a bit more on casting out these particular evil spirits in the session. In particular, he had the afflicted person repeatedly renounce these evil spirits of hopelessness and despair and then the Exorcist commanded them, by name, to leave. We believe that the burden bearer's willingness to take on a bit of the suffering was a spiritual help to the afflicted person. Since the afflicted person was so spiritually weak at that point and, at times overwhelmed, even a mild alleviation of the demonic assault can be critical.

A word of caution is important here. There are some young enthusiastic priests, religious and laity who aspire to such a charism. They want to be victim souls like burden bearers and offer themselves as such. Generally, this is *not* a good idea. Being a burden bearer is a special charism given by God and not usually to be sought out. Such aspirations may actually be more symptomatic of spiritual pride than a true movement of the Spirit. Moreover, it is not for someone new in the spiritual life and should only be done under the guidance of an experienced spiritual director.

Burden bearers are typically those strengthened and purified by years of solid Christian living. Also, they are given special graces to discern the presence of these evil spirits. They are also given special graces to bear up under some intense demonic attacks. But this is only assured when the call to bear such burdens comes from God, not one's own imprudent desires. Normally, dealing with one's own challenges, temptations and burdens is more than enough for a lifetime.

The Occult Third Eye

WE WERE GETTING TO THE END OF THE DEMONIC POSSES-
SION. Most of the demons had left with just the leader
and a small cohort remaining. The leader was greatly
weakened and "on fire." I had been using the "Prayer of
Liberation from the Spirit of Divination" developed by
our friends in the Philippines and found on our app/
website. This was important because the woman had
been involved in witchcraft, as had her mother and other ancestors before her.

It was time to close the "Occult Third Eye." I blessed
her forehead with exorcized oil and prayed three times:
*"Occult Third Eye given by the spirit of divination, I com-
mand you, in the Name of +Jesus to be closed and never to be
opened again."* There was an ear-piercing scream! Wow!
That definitely hit a demonic nerve.

It had been clear throughout the possession that her
Occult Third Eye was opened, that is, she was bonded
to the demons and thus she had access to some of their
thoughts and perceptions, just as they had access to
some of hers. There is a kind of symbiotic relationship
between the demons and a possessed soul.

It appears that some demons actually like to inhabit an incarnate soul. For example, I once commanded a
demon to tell me: "Why don't you leave?" The demon

responded, "I like it here." No doubt it's better than being in hell—although wherever they go, they "take their hell" with them.

In subsequent sessions, we repeated the ritual of closing the third eye. Over the course of the process of closing the third eye (that is—her eye into the demonic world and their eye into hers), the demons texted us several times: "I cannot see or breathe; I am finished." "My eyes are burned to ashes." "I can't breathe Stephen. Doesn't this bother you?" "I cannot see anymore. He took my final eye away." Of course, it is important to take all demonic communications with a grain of salt. They are inveterate liars and manipulators. But occasionally God makes them tell the truth.

Many mediums, spiritualists and occultists claim to have insight into the spiritual world. Some of them actually do, but unfortunately it often comes through the workings of demons. Using a demonic channel only further bonds the user to the Dark World. And whatever you get from such an evil channel is never good.

Recently, I received the following query:

Many years ago when I was doing massage therapy, I used to touch peoples' feet and I could see demons leaving their body. I was working in the New Age world and even worked as a psychic back then. I closed everything down a couple years ago and returned to the Catholic faith. I know I still have these abilities and I'm feeling called to return to healing work with people. I want to do this work now with Jesus, Mary, St. Joseph & the Holy Spirit guiding me.

This woman asked for my opinion about this. She believes she has a healing charism with special "abilities" from God and feels called to use them to help people. She said she would now do it with "Jesus, Mary, St. Joseph and the Holy Spirit" guiding her. Good idea?

Certainly her intentions are good, which one should applaud. However, many an evil has been perpetrated in this world with people intending to do good, such as so-called "good witches." Regardless of one's intentions, there is no good witchcraft.

In this case, great caution is warranted, which was communicated to her. A few people do have a real healing charism from God including seeing demons and assisting in casting them out, although it is relatively rare. However, this woman has a significant history of New Age spiritualities including working as a psychic! As noted previously, some practitioners of the occult do have special "abilities" but they come from demons and/or the opening of their occult third eye.

In this person's case, it would be prudent to assume her "abilities" come from the dark world and not from God. It can take 3-4 years of solid Catholic living, including regular confession and deliverance prayers, before the demonic effects of years of occult practice are "scrubbed out." This includes a final closing of the occult third eye.

I recommended to her that she engage in ongoing deliverance prayers for herself and continued sacramental living. If she becomes involved in a healing ministry too early, knowingly or not using the occult third eye, she would likely become a channel for spiritual deception and harm.

People underestimate the evil wrought by practicing the occult. What is the harm? It is a violation of the First Commandment against God, and its spiritual devastation should not be underestimated. While a good confession indeed wipes out the sin, the evil *effects* of such sins are typically not immediately and fully expunged, a theological principle well understood by the Catholic faith.

We have a safe and holy means to access the Triune God and the heavens: prayer in Jesus. In Him, we usually do not get the tantalizing knowledge that we might want. But we need to trust that whatever the Lord chooses to give us, it is what we should have. Whatever the Lord gives is always for our benefit and contributes to our happiness. Jesus, I trust in you!

Gaslighted
by Demons

MORE WEIRD THINGS HAVE BEEN HAPPENING TO OUR COMPUTERS AND IT IS MAKING ME A LITTLE "CRAZY." Our IT expert is experiencing unusual problems trying to update our app, which he has never encountered. In the midst of the online sessions, our computers have inexplicably shut down; our batteries drained down even though they were plugged into a wall socket; our rapid internet connection slowed down to a crawl, and more. I have come to expect that with EVERY online session, there will be some new IT wrinkle that cannot be explained naturally.

The latest inexplicable IT event is that I cannot access our own website, and other SMC related sites, no matter what browser, which computer, or what internet provider I use. I had to go to a local coffee shop to post the last blog which then went out this week without a hitch.

It is becoming clear that demons are again harassing us and trying to shut down our online deliverance ministry. And they are trying to mess with our minds. They are trying to assert control, confuse and disempower us, and make us think we are a little crazy (it's working! Hah!). In short, they are gaslighting us. Recently having become aware of what the term: "gaslighting" means,[11] I suggest that demons are the original gaslighters. Literally, they invented it.

Demons gaslight our clients as well. There are many people who are mentally ill and erroneously believe they have demons. We refer them to mental health professionals. But there are also people who are not mentally ill and do have demons. In the process of liberation, after months of clear demonic manifestations, some have told me that they think that they do not have demons and they are just "crazy." One possessed person even said to me, somewhat ironically: "The demons told me that I am not possessed and that I am just crazy." Wow! It seemed that she was actually inclined to believe them!

Demons also gaslight people by psychologically manipulating them to break down their self-esteem and self-confidence. They sow doubts and mental confusion. They try to establish power and control over people. Demons are masters of gaslighting and clearly are its original authors. Satan is the "Father of Lies"; he is also the "Father of Gaslighting."

The key is to recognize when you are being mentally manipulated by demons and reject it. I recommend saying the 3 R's: I reject it, I rebuke it, I renounce it. I recently received an email from one of our subscribers affirming this approach:

My family and I have been partaking in the monthly deliverance sessions for two years and they've been life changing. I personally adopted the 3Rs "Reject, rebuke and renounce" any evil spirit oppressing me. But recently (2 weeks ago), I had a powerful experience with it. I came back from work feeling a little off/depressed and didn't make much of it. I thought it was just the weight of the day. However, the dark thoughts got more pressing as I was getting ready for work the next day. A voice in my head kept saying: "Don't you see how ugly you look; your hair is mess; don't go to work, stay home and kill yourself!"

I felt so heavy...but in a flash I remembered your talk about demon brain and told myself: "Those are NOT your thoughts! Cast out the evil right now." I stood in the middle of my bedroom and started the 3Rs prayer out loud: "In the Holy Name of Jesus Christ, by the power of His most Precious Blood & Glorious Cross, price of my redemption, I..." But nothing was coming out, my voice had died!

I started over, but the same thing—when I got to the part where I'm to reject, renounce and rebuke, I became silent. I called on the Holy Spirit and started over a 3rd time. This time, I made it through the entire prayer. I felt a chilly sensation go through my body right after. I went to work and about my day with no feeling of depression or dark thoughts.

I am aware of the battles the team at SMC is facing, and wanted you to know how much your ministry is touching lives, changing lives through Jesus Christ! May God continue to bless you and the ministry.

There are many important takeaways in her experience. First, when "demon brain" hits us or demons manipulate us in other ways, we usually don't immediately recognize the work of the Evil One. This woman finally did, perhaps with a special grace from heaven. Second, her explicit rejection of these evil thoughts was very helpful. She used the 3 R's: I reject them; I rebuke them; I renounce them. Third, she initially could not even speak. It took three tries! The Evil One does everything he can to block our holy acts including blocking our voice, fogging our brains, and putting many obstacles in our paths. Fourth, the depression and dark thoughts lifted as a result of her prayer. This confirms that the mental attacks were indeed of a demonic origin and not simply due to her own human failings.

Not everyone who uses this prayer will experience such a swift and dramatic release. But all of us regularly suffer demonic temptations until the end of our days. If we hold out to the end, trusting in Jesus and rejecting the voice of the Evil One, it will be a source of great sanctification. These trials will help make us the saints that God wants us to be.

So, when unusual things start happening, instead of thinking that I am a bit "crazy," I try to recognize when demons are gaslighting us and I use the three R's too. Plus, I try to prepare to make sure our ministry and sessions are successful. For example, if the demons are messing with my technology, I try redundancy. At times, multiple ways of our team contacting a possessed client are necessary; the demons may block one avenue but not another. Also, having redundant IT platforms is likewise key. For example, one week's blog post was done on a backup computer using an internet hotspot. The main computer and internet link were inexplicably inoperable.

Most of all, I must trust in Jesus. It is our consistent experience that the demons can only harass but not destroy. Moreover, the fact that the demons are working overtime to stop our ministry is a back-handed demonic "compliment": our ministry is spiritually important enough for hell to employ significant resources to try to stop it. Demons can make our ministry challenging, but this ministry is God's work and He will give us a way to accomplish it. Similarly, while demons can gaslight the possessed, they, too, need to look to Jesus and trust in him.

In stark contrast to gaslighting, God loves, affirms, supports and encourages. He respects the free will He gave us and does not attempt to control or manipulate. Rather, He invites us into his healing and love. His message to us is that we are loved, we are forgiven, and that we are beautifully made in His image.

Dogs and Demons

I LOVE DOGS. I grew up with one and she was a wonderful influence on our family...I recall an encounter with demons some time ago when I was commanding them to be obedient. Each time they disobeyed, I sprayed them with holy water. I explained to a team member present that dealing with demons is like dealing with disobedient beasts: they had to be trained.

At that point, the demons clearly felt insulted and offended. They spoke up and said: "I am not a dog!" I responded, "No, you are not! You don't deserve the name of a dog. They are kind, obedient and loving. You are NONE of these things. You don't deserve to be called a dog." The demons' response? Silence.

In our exorcism ministry, we occasionally experience the salutary effects of dogs, for example, in the case of a young woman who was possessed and also had a history of drug abuse. It began in her infancy with her mother, a cocaine addict and a witch, who admittedly put cocaine and other drugs into her baby formula to "control her." The mother also dedicated her to Satan. Shortly thereafter the mother died in her 20's. The daughter was adopted and eventually, after a personal battle of several years including extensive exorcisms, was free of drugs and liberated from the Evil One.

But the history of severe early drug abuse took its toll. Her mental and relational abilities were limited. She had difficulty making healthy friendships and was spending too much time alone. This made her more vulnerable to relapsing with drugs and more vulnerable to demonic manipulation.

Wisely, her adoptive father got her a dog. She loves the dog and often texts pictures of her and her dog together. They are inseparable. Her Dad said, "Best idea I've had was to rescue the dog." He added: "So she has a routine and is learning responsibility [with the dog] and it gives her emotional support as well." The dog has also given her an emotional stability she never had, which is very helpful in her long-term freedom from demons and drugs.

The demons recognize the salutary effects of the dog and they are *very* angry. After her liberation, they have been trying desperately to get her back and one obstacle is the dog. They angrily texted in capital letters: "SHE WAS NEVER SUPPOSED TO HELP FIND THAT DOG." A peaceful, contented soul is not likely to welcome in some demons and they know it.

Another woman who had an encounter with demons sent me this personal witness:

Years ago when I was about 14 yrs old, I played the ouija board with a couple of friends. We asked it for signs and questions of that nature. Needless to say, it gave signs. That night I went home. I sat down after warming up my dinner with my back to the window with my dog, a mixed Scottish terrier, at my feet. All of a sudden my dog was slightly growling and when I looked down at him, he was not looking at me, but looking over my left shoulder past me towards the window. His growl got louder and he bared his teeth. I was getting scared myself because I didn't know why he was acting like that. All of a sudden his hair stood straight up! At that very moment, I remember getting chills all over and I stood halfway up and quickly looked back at the window. What I saw almost dropped me with fear. I saw a face with an elongated nose, defined protruding cheeks, and a pointed chin with a grin that was exaggerated. I jumped away from the table as my dog lunged with a fierceness as if he was going to fight another dog. He leaped past me barring his canines and barking, but the bark was deep and intense. I looked back and the demon was gone. As scared as I was, I remember my Mom always telling me to invoke the name of Jesus when in fear. So I kept saying: "In the name of Jesus I command you to leave" and I ran to the back door, let my dog out who was now scratching at the door to go after whatever was in the back yard. It was about 9 o'clock at night. The backyard seemed darker than usual especially as I couldn't see my dog and all I could hear was his barking. As astounding as all this sounds, I say it was a demon because its skin color was deep orange. I know many won't believe me on this, but his skin had a deep orange hue. My dog saw it first, warned me and then went to my defense to protect me. This is a true story, I use it to warn young people, not to ever ever play the ouija board. I went to a Catholic school and the nuns always warned us not to play the ouija board, as well as my mother. But being a curious kid, I knew it was wrong, but I played it that one time anyway. Lesson learned.

Her story is interesting and instructive for a few reasons. First, playing with divination, including ouija boards, is a very bad idea. It is not a harmless game and there can be some ugly consequences which our clients have repeatedly shared with us. This girl did it once and a demon showed up. God gave her the "grace" to see it and to stop this dangerous practice. Had she continued in such divination (e.g. mediums, tarot cards, seances) she would most probably have become possessed.

The girl's experience regarding her brave dog is also heart-warming. The dog saw the demon and recognized the threat. Courageously, the dog leapt into action and lunged after it. We have had several other experiences of dogs seeing demons and valiantly trying to protect their people. For example, in one case of a demonically infested house, the family dog would sit at the bedroom door to protect the family at night. It would howl in an alarming pitch when the demons approached. I do not know if all dogs can see demons, but I am completely convinced some can and I have had solid experiences of this.

While dogs can warn us, I have not found them helpful in actually chasing demons away. Dogs do not have such power, but Jesus does. Thankfully the girl's Mother had told her to invoke Jesus' holy name when in fear, which she did. Wise counsel. The demon was cast out.

Over the years, I have witnessed and read story after story of how an animal, especially a dog, has been a wonderful grace in someone's life. Each of us has a guardian angel who watches over us 24/7. I think they sometimes intervene in our lives with a little, four-footed helper.

Demons and Sex

DEMONS DO NOT HAVE BODIES. They are pure spirits. They cannot literally have sex with someone and impregnate them, even though they will sometimes threaten women with doing so. One ancient source thought that demons could take real male sperm from another person and put it into a woman and thus impregnate her. However, I have never witnessed anything remotely approaching such and personally I do not believe it.

However, demons can manipulate people's minds, especially those who are willing and/or are fully possessed. They can simulate experiences in people's minds and these individuals will swear it is real. For example, during one exorcism, a mother and I plus the Team were praying over a young woman—her daughter. At the end of the session, the afflicted young woman came back to consciousness and said emphatically to me, "You stabbed my hand with a knife!" Whereupon the mother said that this did not happen. Moreover, the young woman did not have a wound in her hand nor did I have a knife. But the demons simulated the experience in her mind and, to her, it was very real.

A man contacted me a while ago and said that he is "in love" with his guardian angel and that they have sex daily. My immediate thought was this person was mentally unbalanced. However, demons can simulate sexual intercourse in someone's mind and demons do often disguise themselves as someone's guardian angel. So, it is entirely possible that this man is regularly having simulated sex with a demon, thinking it is his guardian angel. If true, such a man is in deep spiritual trouble. Any sort of relationship with a demon is very bad; a sexual relationship with one is of the gravest import.

Demons, like all angels, are not broken down into male and female. While they can be represented as male to portray a strong warrior spirit, they are not male. Some are portrayed as more feminine to suggest more stereotypical feminine qualities. But, as pure spirits, they do not have gender.

It is common to speak of incubus and succubus spirits. Incubus spirits take the form of a male to seduce women and succubus spirits seduce men. I know of a woman who said she was sexually stimulated by demons every night. She said she wanted to reject them but was lacking in will power. She was referred to a solid spiritual director to assist her.

Demons try to sexually seduce men and women in a variety of ways. Most commonly it is done through the *ordinary* demonic means of tempting them through the actions of other human beings and/or pornography and the like. However, there are *extraordinary* demonic interventions which can sexually tempt humans.

Sadly, one common occurrence in an exorcism is the "raping" of a possessed female. Women are especially shamed by forced sexual encounters. Demons know this and will not uncommonly "rape" a woman during an exorcism, or at other times. This has happened very often for fully possessed women, although sometimes with men as well. It is a terrible trial.

The demons do this first simply because they are vicious creatures that take delight in torturing humans. Second, they will often try to bargain with the individual: "If you stop going to these exorcisms, I will leave you alone." Of course, this is a lie. Third, they will simulate raping the individual during an exorcism and then taunt the Exorcist: "See what you made me do!" They will blame their actions on the Exorcist, hoping to stop the exorcisms.

Some people say God wouldn't allow such a thing—demons raping young women. In fact, God does indeed allow such things, just as He allows human beings to viciously rape other human beings including children. It says less about God and more about the depravity of humans and demons.

I have tried to help women who are undergoing this trial by explaining that, although their minds tell them they are being raped, demons do not have bodies and so it is not actually true, no matter how real it feels. I don't know how consoling this is, because the horrible experience feels so real.

This is yet another reason why we ALWAYS have a woman team member present during an exorcism of another woman. Demons will sexually harass the energumen in many ways. One of those is to convince the person that a team member, usually the Exorcist, is raping the person. So, I am careful never to see an afflicted female alone. If they need to go to confession, they should confess to their parish priest.

I have had several cases where the demons induced the afflicted woman to think I was raping her. In one case, it was particularly absurd since, at the time, she was hundreds of miles away. But she was convinced, as a result of the demonic manipulation of her mind, that I was raping her. Our extra caution and sometimes rather "rigid" boundaries with the possessed are necessary.

This exorcism ministry is complex and fraught with dangers. This is why an exorcist should be a senior priest, with years of experience, specifically trained as an exorcist, working within a team context, and maintaining clear and protective boundaries for all. This is probably one of the most important teachings I pass on to new exorcists in training.

Satan's Seductions: Exorcists Beware!

SATAN DOES INDEED TRY TO MANIPULATE, SEDUCE AND CORRUPT HUMANS VIA SEXUALITY. It is one of his most constant ploys during an exorcism. A majority of the possessed are women and typically fairly young. All priest-exorcists are male. As every senior exorcist has experienced, Satan will try to derail the process and the Exorcist's ministry using sexual means. (Of course, it can also happen with male clients but most commonly with females.)

The list of sexual advances and overtures exorcists have experienced in exorcisms is very long. It is important to note that these happen most often when the afflicted person is manifesting the demonic in some way and thus not in complete control, or often not even conscious. Rather it is the demons who are acting and, after the event, many of the afflicted are not even aware of what took place and are often embarrassed to learn of it.

Just a few of the sexual events exorcists have experienced include:

- One woman showed up for an exorcism and said, "I have sexual demons." She was dressed very seductively. She was informed of the proper dress code for future sessions and wrapped in a blanket for that day's session.

- A young woman, with a long history of sexual sins and abuse, would often seductively lick her fingers during a session and whisper seductive invitations to the Exorcist.

- Many women report feeling strong sexual impulses toward the Exorcist which are out of character and suggest a demonic source.

- In the midst of a session, the manifesting energumen simulated sexual behaviors.

- One young woman told the Exorcist: "I have demons on my panties" and another very visibly reached into her bra and pulled out a note to read to the priest.

- Afflicted women repeatedly calling the priest late at night crying for his help and his prayers to help them "sleep."

While reading these might be a bit disturbing to some, they are very typical of what happens repeatedly in an exorcism and needs to be said out loud. Publicly exposing Satan's wiles is an important step in overcoming his plans.

As noted, many times the women involved are embarrassed if they find out what transpired. Some are more vulnerable to demonic sexual manipulation because of the poor sexual boundaries they learned by being sexually abused as a minor. All are being used by Satan to foil the Exorcist.

Satan would be very pleased if the Exorcist succumbed to these temptations and had a sexual relationship with the afflicted woman. Sadly, this has happened in more than one case. However, Satan's goals are usually more subtle. If he can derail the focus and prayers of the Exorcist, this will help to make the sessions less effective. Causing the Exorcist and/or team members to entertain impure thoughts and/or lust is very effective in derailing an exorcism and actually fuels the demons present.

Moreover, if Satan can create an unhealthy soul-tie between the afflicted woman and the priest, then a dangerous situation can develop. This can slowly, subtly happen if the Exorcist and afflicted person have ongoing, individual private contact for an extended basis. Such a situation is ripe for developing unhealthy soul-ties: many afflicted women have been sexually abused as a minor; the afflicted woman often feels alone and frightened; she may crave the protection and attention of a strong male figure; she abandons herself into the care of this male figure. The Exorcist, for his part, will work closely with her for months, perhaps years. He will know her inner fears and vulnerabilities. He will likely develop an affection for this suffering soul. If he has some weaknesses around setting good boundaries and/or a savior complex, he will be very vulnerable.

What to do? Our Team has developed some important boundaries which we have found very effective:

- If clients come inappropriately dressed, they are wrapped in a blanket for the session and instructed to dress more modestly in the future.

- Clients who start making sexual gyrations during a session are also wrapped in a blanket for the session.

- Female clients are given a trained female staff member/volunteer to communicate with between sessions. They do not communicate with the Exorcist.

- All exorcism sessions with females must have a female present or a family member. All sessions with males must have another person present.

- Priest-exorcists do not touch the client during sessions except to lay hands on their heads at the appropriate time or to lay their stoles on the necks of the afflicted person. If the afflicted person needs personal assistance, one of the lay women will help.

- Priest-exorcists never meet with the clients privately– ever. If pastoral counseling, support or other pastoral needs surface, the client will speak to our trained female lay team member or contact their local parish.

While such boundaries might appear overly rigid, they have been critical for the Center's safety and well-being, and that of the afflicted. It has lifted a huge weight off my shoulders as an exorcist and empowered our laity in roles more suited to their gifts.

I cannot express how grateful I am to our gifted and faith-filled team members. They have been a great blessing for me and I know the Lord will return to them 100-fold.

An Exorcism is a Knife Fight

As an Air Force veteran, I am familiar a bit with modern combat. It has become very impersonal and distant. Missiles are hurled at the enemy from miles away. Bombs are dropped from high altitude. Now, drones are remotely piloted, and targets are attacked from great distances. We no longer see the enemy's face.

Not so in an exorcism. An exorcism is more akin to a knife fight. We move into close contact with demons. Our "weapons" of holy water, a crucifix, relics of the saints, and the prayers of the Church are used in immediate contact with the demons. We are within arms' reach of each other. In one case, the energumen, fully manifesting, reached out and tried to strangle me.

We see the face of the demons, appearing on the person's face, right in front of us. Their look of pure evil, hatred, and violence is disconcerting. As noted earlier, part of the actual discernment of whether someone is possessed is precisely in this personal encounter of the Exorcist with the afflicted person. He looks for many typical signs and he also "feels" the evil presence of the demons. Being only a few feet away from such a viciously evil entity, a sensitive exorcist will feel it.

After such an intense encounter and battle with evil, I am tired, drained of energy. One new exorcist asked me about this. When he finishes a session, he is abnormally tired and wondered if it was normal. It is. It is a kind of spiritual tiredness which is very real.

In addition to feeling tired, I often feel a bit "slimed" by the presence of such evil. And I feel a bit wounded. We say cleansing prayers at the end of each session which helps considerably. But sometimes, a second round of cleansing prayers is needed, especially with difficult cases. Nevertheless, it's hard to get rid of all the demonic "slime."

In the military, I remember undergoing a training session on knife fighting. I don't recall much of the specifics but the one thing I do recall is a striking sentence from the Instructor: "In a knife fight, you will get cut." If you lose, you die. But even if you win, you will get cut.

This is how an exorcism feels. It feels like close-in, hand-to-hand combat. I walk away, celebrating the victory of Christ over the demons. But I am cut. After three intense exorcisms in one day, I spend some time lying down and recuperating, even after having said all the cleansing prayers. In a knife fight, you get cut.

I also know that some nights, in the midst of working with someone with a strong demonic presence, the person's demons will attack me. The more powerful the demons possessing the person, the stronger the attacks. We do not tell possessed people about these attacks. We would not burden them with such knowledge. It's an accepted part of our ministry.

Actually, the presence of these attacks confirms that the person is truly possessed. And the type of attacks lets us know what kind of demons are possessing the person. I also believe that undergoing a little bit of what is oppressing the afflicted person is a grace and is an aid to his/her eventual liberation, and noted in the chapter on burden bearers. So, it is not always bad that we get attacked.

Accepting someone for an exorcism is a huge commitment. There is a kind of "soul" commitment the Exorcist implicitly makes with the afflicted person: "I will fight for you. I will face the Evil One with you. I will get slimed and cut. I will descend into the darkness with you; I will persevere and not abandon you, even when it seems hopeless. We will walk this journey together."

I do not make such a commitment lightly. I want to be morally certain the person is truly possessed and also a good candidate for an exorcism. For example, if they will not be obedient and follow our instructions, and if they will not practice the faith and amend their lives as needed, the exorcism will fail. If I am going to get "cut," I can only take so many of these encounters. I am limited in the number of people I can personally accompany. I need to parse myself out to those who will truly benefit.

Some say that exorcists die young. I have not found this to be true. For example, the Jesuit exorcists who performed the famous exorcism on the 13-year-old young person, which is loosely recounted in the haunting 1970's movie "The Exorcist," died a ripe old age. I expect to do so as well. However, a priest who engages in this ministry full time, and not the occasional case, will be changed. Repeatedly looking at the face of Evil, being slimed daily, and daily enduring its onslaughts changes a man. After living in the preternatural world for years, one cannot go back to a comfortable life in the mundane. While God heals and protects, the Exorcist is nonetheless changed.

The Exorcist's focus is in the preternatural world. He is a friend of the angels and the foe of the demons. The saints intercede for him; Satan is out to destroy him. He breathes the air of the angels more than that the earth.

At times, he is choked by the fetid smoke of hell. The Virgin Mary spreads her mantle over him.

I could not imagine being reassigned after this ministry to a typical parish assignment. This is something bishops should consider—after years of full-time exorcisms, a priest may no longer be suitable for a regular assignment. Perhaps it is best to assign old priests as exorcists and when they are finished casting out demons, they need to retire. However, I don't plan to retire but rather to die in place, God willing. It is a fight to the end. An exorcist-priest never really stops being an exorcist.

Demons Texting

Of all that I share with individuals about this ministry, one of the most intriguing for many individuals, and often disbelieved, is the idea that I get text messages from demons. Actually, I get A LOT of them. In conversations with other exorcists around the country, I am not the only one. Exorcists with an active caseload typically report receiving, at some point, texts from demons.[12] Typically the texts appear to be coming from the phone of the possessed but, when the phone is checked, these texts do not appear. In one set of demonic texts, the phone number listed for the source was: "000 666."

Demonic texts typically come from bigger cases where there are higher-ranking demons. I suspect it takes a higher-ranking demon to break into the physical world and send text messages. Demons are not omnipotent and they only have a limited amount of spiritual energy. It likely takes quite a bit of energy for them to text on a regular basis. Since their abilities are limited, they focus their finite energy according to Satan's plan. (Yes, he does have a plan as noted previously, but it is doomed to fail. All evil is inherently self-defeating and self-destructive.) They will only do so when there is much at stake, from their perspective.

That demons would text makes perfect sense. In the past, they messed with electronic devices of all sorts such as televisions, radios and lights—turning them on and off to scare people. They would also slam doors and windows. They throw objects across the room.

Now there are computers and new forms of communication for them to manipulate. Some time ago, I had videotaped a particularly difficult exorcism session and sat down to view the tape. This was the first time I had ever watched a tape of one of my sessions. At the very end of the viewing, my computer screen went berserk. It flashed all sorts of messages I had never seen and then shut down. It was a new computer. I took it to a technician and the IT person said the hard drive was completely and inexplicably fried. He exclaimed, "What did you do to this?" I knew exactly what happened to it: no doubt the demons were not happy to listen to themselves scream and undergo excruciating pain in an exorcism. For protection, I now take a sticker with a Benedictine medal and put it on the computer

In the 21st century, cell phones are everywhere. Demons, being the gadget freaks they are, derive delight in tormenting and harassing people on these electronic phones. I suspect one of the reasons people balk at the idea of demons texting is that receiving text messages is something very immediate and personal in their lives. It is a frightening thought that demons can intrude so personally and so concretely. It makes the reality of demons more immediate and thus more frighteningly real than we would like to admit.

I specifically recall three particularly striking cases in which demons have texted the team and/or the family of the possessed person. Two of these cases were the most difficult cases we have had so far, and the third involved a pious family with a priestly vocation among the children. So, all were "high value" targets with high-ranking, powerful demons involved. Below is a small sample of the verbatim texts we received in these cases, minus some of the particularly vile and unrepeatable demonic comments:

CASE 1   Demonic texts Received by Possessed Young Woman's Priest-spiritual Director:

Demons: *"Her torments start now, priest...all night. While you and that friend of yours* [the priest exorcist] *sleep...We will make her bleed. We're glad she's away from you now."*

"Be ready. We're coming for you and the girl."

Priest texts back: "Be gone in the name of Jesus!

Demons: *"Stop. She'll die."* ... *"Kill her. Come on priest. Do it. If you don't, we will. We want her dead."*

Priest: "Vade retro Satanas." (Get behind me Satan).

Demons: *"Stop."*

Priest: "Blood of Jesus splashed on you."

Demons: *"Stop it. We'll hurt her more."* ... *"We hate you. Stop leading her."*

"There is no power in the priesthood." ...

"You are weak. You know there's nothing you can do to help her. And you've given up. You sleep, she'll scream."

Priest: "You are crushed by Our Lady's heel. Vade (depart)!"

Demons: *"Stop. Let us have our fun."*

Priest: "Forbidden, foul fiend!"

Demons: *"We're abusing her. She's better off dead. Let her go....She can't handle the sexual and physical abuse."*

Priest: "Leave."

Demons: *"We're not leaving."*

CASE 2 Demonic Texts Received by Mother of Possessed Young Woman:

Demons: *"Don't worry. I'll take care of her."*

"There's nothing more you can do to help her. You have tried to help her, but you have failed. You have failed at it. There is no more time for helping, only waiting and watching. She is in good hands...you can't protect her from us."

"Just so you know it's going to be interesting ... you won't know when we will come but we will and you just won't believe it all...let's have some fun."

CASE 3 Demonic Texts Received by Father of Possessed Young Woman:

Demons: *"My baby and I are going to have a fun night... [you] should have protected her more."*

"You are going to give up, you are going to get worn down. You'll lose patience. She's mine."

"Say goodbye to your baby soon....You don't know who I am but I'm coming for your baby."

"She's mine."

It is interesting that in Case 3, a friend of the possessed young woman was in the room with her and she said, "It's [the demon] talking to her. I heard it. Now it's laughing....Her phone is down but screen is lighting up." The friend said she actually audibly heard the demon's voice in the room and saw the phone typing out a text message with no human touching the keys.

In these texts in three unrelated cases, we get a sense of the common demonic personality. They act like immature adolescents who are electronic gadget freaks. They are narcissistic, arrogant and boastful. They constantly threaten, denigrate and put us down with demeaning words. They are sadists who describe their torments and tortures of others as "fun."

But their words and actions are never haphazard. They always have a specific goal. A major goal in these cases was to dissuade and discourage those supporting the possessed person. Their words indirectly tell us of the importance of the support of others. The possessed are buoyed up and helped greatly by their parents and friends. These are important connections which the demons try to break. Like wolves attacking a flock, they try to isolate a wounded sheep and then move in for the kill.

Also, these demonic texts inadvertently affirm that the prayers of the priest are effective and there is great power in the priesthood. Demons often tell the priest to "stop" the prayers and threaten retaliation.

All three individuals, by the grace of God, have been liberated. The demons did everything they could to convince the priests and the family to abandon them. But their loved ones did not waiver nor did the love of Christ. Ultimately, Love cast them out.

Mary, Mother of Exorcists

I HAVE NEVER HEARD OF JESUS PERSONALLY SHOWING UP IN AN EXORCISM AND CASTING OUT THE DEMONS. Perhaps it has happened but I have not yet heard of it. Every other exorcist I have discussed this point with has the same experience.

Of course, it is in Jesus' holy name that the demons are cast out. Recently, a possessed person told me that whenever I say the holy name of Jesus, it makes the demons "seriously angry" and he finds it "very painful." Jesus' death and resurrection is THE fundamental exorcism that smashed Satan's kingdom. The name and power of Christ casts out demons. So then why doesn't He personally show up at exorcisms?

Understanding who Satan is and thus his punishment is important. Satan tried to make himself equal to God. As one of our exorcism prayers addresses Satan, "In your great pride you still presume to be held equal [to God]." One might speculate that if Jesus, the God-man, were to show up in person to cast out Satan, it would support Satan's delusions that he can be on the same plane as God, to challenge Him, and to be equal to Him. But Satan is dust compared to Jesus; he is a lowly creature who has made himself even lower because of his evil.

Moreover, it is often speculated by theologians that one of the reasons Satan originally rebelled against God

was in response to the revelation of the Incarnation. For
Satan, it was an insult that God would choose to exalt
our lowly humanity instead of his superior angelic nature. Satan's pride and envy blinded him and he became
enraged against Jesus and all of humanity, perpetually
dedicated to destroying it.

In response, Jesus sends a "lowly" woman from the
Middle East to cast him out. Her only "weapons" are
her love for Jesus, her total humility, and her obedience
to God. It is precisely in these that we humans triumph
over evil. According to Divine justice, Satan is enduring a truth he never learned: the essence of true power
belonging to our humble, loving, self-sacrificing God.
As St. Paul says: "I will rather boast most gladly of my
weaknesses, in order that the power of Christ may dwell
with me" (2 Cor 12:9).

I personally believe that the leadership of the ministry of exorcism has been delegated by God to the Blessed Virgin Mary, one of the humble human beings Satan
hates most. She is the Mother of Exorcists. I believe she
is spiritually present at every exorcism. She often makes
her presence directly felt in casting out Satan.

Recently, one of our exorcists was in a difficult session. He wanted to make the demons face the truth,
which is very painful and odious for them, and exorcistic. It is especially effective when they face the truth
about the Virgin Mary. He commanded them, "Tell me
the truth. In the holy name of Jesus: What is the most
majestic of Our Lady's titles?" They refused to answer:
"I can't say!" "Why not?" he responded. The demons
said, "It burns me." The Exorcist said, "I command you
to say it!" The demonic response, "Mother!" "Mother of
what?" he demanded. Then with a look of complete de-

spair and weeping, the demons said, "Mother of God."
The demons were in agony to say it.

Similarly, in another session, the Exorcist commanded the demons to answer the question, "Is the Virgin
Mary beautiful?" "NO, NO, NO!" they screamed. He insisted, "In Jesus' name, tell the truth: Is she beautiful?"
With a look of despair, awe and hatred, they begrudg-
ingly said, "She is the most beautiful creature in all of
creation." And then the demons let out a scream. While
we are always cautious about believing anything demons say, since they are inveterate liars, they are sometimes forced by God to tell the truth.

Mary, the Immaculate, carries within her the presence of her Son Jesus. She carries Jesus in her heart. She
is the true "Ark of the Covenant." She is the perfect dis-
ciple and thus the presence of Christ in her is power-
fully exorcistic. The demons cannot stand being in her
humble, obedient, holy presence. They cannot even say
her name without it causing great, great pain.

Some time ago, we were in a very tough case. The
young woman was possessed by hundreds of demons
with Satan himself personally leading them. But the
more difficult the case, the stronger the graces God
gives. In this case, I knew that we would need the very
best God could send. We were coming close to the end,
after countless hours of ugly and painful sessions. The
demons were getting weaker and were now more obedient, much to their dismay. I commanded them, in the
name of Jesus, to tell us: "When will you leave and by
what means?" The demons reluctantly responded with
a date two weeks hence and said, "She will come." Everyone in the room knew who "she" was. The demons

would not say the name of the Mother of God. Her name, like that of her Son, is itself holy.

The day finally came and the moment approached. The room grew silent and the possessed woman said, "She is here." As the Virgin quietly moved closer, the demons began to thrash wildly. She said nothing but the radiant light of Christ shining through the humble handmaid of God was overpowering. Satan himself screamed. After screaming and thrashing several times, the Prince of Darkness left. It was over.

Now, I ask all of the possessed to consecrate themselves to the Mother of God as part of the healing process. We ask Mary not only to cast out the demons but to protect the afflicted person for the rest of their lives, until she welcomes them into the Kingdom. The Gates of Hell will not prevail against the Church, or against its Mother.

I do not know a seasoned exorcist who does not have a deep, heart-felt devotion to the Mother of God. In fact, I tell new exorcists in training that such a devotion is not simply a pious addition to one's ministry. It is essential. We begin every exorcism invoking the aid of the most powerful Mother of God. As the Rite of Exorcism reminds Satan of his eternal torment: "From the first moment of her Immaculate Conception, she crushed your proud head!"

Coughing Up Demons

"C" WAS REPEATEDLY CURSED BY WITCHES AND IS NOW DEMONICALLY AFFLICTED. A couple of nights ago, she received a threatening text from demons: "You'll have your migraine all night for throwing me up b...[expletive]." A few hours prior to the text, C was being greatly oppressed by demons so we prayed over her. Then she vomited up an ugly, thick, black liquid. Some demons departed and she returned to full self-consciousness.

Preternatural coughing and vomiting during an exorcism are typically a positive development. They are a sign that demons are being cast out. In the demonic text, the demons admitted that she vomited them up and they were threatening to give her a migraine in retaliation. Similarly, in the case of a man who is the subject of daily curses by an angry witch, he coughs and has the dry heaves for a few minutes whenever exorcism prayers are said and, in particular, the lifting of curses, and only then.

We have long known that, in the final stages of liberation, the afflicted will often vomit up strange things. Exorcists have reported unusual objects being ejected such as nails, chains, demonic figurines, cursed objects, and even snakes. These items were not in the afflicted person's stomach but rather preternaturally materialized in the throat and mouth.

The object in the vomit will be related to the cause and/or substance of their possession. It is not random. In this case, C was cursed by a witch. What she coughed up was a kind of witches' bolus or substance of the curse. Given the substance and amount of the black liquid she continually coughed up, it must be preternatural otherwise she would be dead.

We have other folks who are also suffering from witches' curses or evil spirits of divination. Some of them have also excreted ugly substances from various bodily orifices. This can be a bit embarrassing but we assure the person that it is not unusual and it is a positive step forward. After the excretion, afflicted persons always say they feel lighter and freer.

There is a related prayer for exorcists on our app/ website, "Prayer for Someone Who Has Ingested a Cursed Object," which concludes with:

> "I exorcise you so that all evil should be destroyed and annihilated in whatever manner it was done to the servant of God N. Pass from his (her) visceral organs and push the evil out, so that you will be spitted out naturally without damaging his (her) body or mind. Amen."[13]

Witches' curses are very real. Some have claimed that the curses only have power if the person who is the object of the curse believes in them. But this has not been our experience. In one case, the cursed victim said to me, "I would never have believed what the witch is able to do to me and my family." Their curses invoke the dark power of demons.

A converted sorcerer and former practitioner of witchcraft said that witchcraft is a "power trip." Satan seduces the beginner with a feeling of power. The curses have an effect, although unbeknown to the person it is Satan who is pulling the strings and not the witch. Through the work of demons, he gives the person an increasing experience of power and thus reels the practitioner into his clutches. In reality, it is Satan who is in control and the witch is merely a pawn and minion of the Evil One.

Moreover, it is always important to remember that curses are nothing compared to the liberating power of Christ. As noted earlier, I once commanded the demons to tell me: "Who is Lord: Jesus or Satan? I command you to tell the truth!" The demons snarled and choked out the truth. They said, "Jesus."

Perhaps the most intriguing items someone coughed up in one of our exorcisms was a bunch (maybe 6-9) of little flowers. Since such items are part of the curse we considered them unholy and cursed and thus we quickly disposed of them. However, a team member took pictures and we tried to identify this unusual looking little flower. It turned out, through an internet search, perhaps to be a match of a West African plant called a *Rinorea oblongifolia*. "Strange," we thought, "Why this one?"

The head possessing demon claimed, with a sneer and smirk, that this was his "seed" placed in her. The entire case of possession had strong sexual overtones and the head demon claimed her as his sex slave. He said he had a special place for her in hell with him. The young woman was especially vulnerable to sexual demons because of her sordid sexual past with multiple rapes and numerous sexual partners. She also had a tattoo on her leg of a flower which turned out to be a huge demonic portal. Whenever we threw holy water on it, the demons screamed.

But why a West African flower? We recall that the objects coughed up in an exorcism are related to the Evil One's hold on the person. The flower symbolized her sexuality. But I recalled that some of the occult which came to America came from people abducted from West Africa. They brought with them their native Voodoo which eventually was melded into Santeria, Palo, and other Western Hemisphere occult practices.

So, our hypothesis is that the flowers represented both the sexual connection with the Evil One and the occult. In fact, the head possessing demon said that the flowers were his "seed" planted in her. Of course, demons, of themselves have no sexuality since, as angels, they do not have bodies or gender. However, they do prey upon the sexual vulnerabilities of humans and gleefully manipulate and sexually torture them, as the demon in this case often did.

The portal that was the tattoo was nullified through months of cleansing with holy water and deliverance prayers. Moreover, this young woman, having been the object of many evil curses, coughed up a number of boluses, in addition to the flowers. Again and again, she coughed up a lot of an ugly black slime, indicative of how extensive the curses levied against her. But, by the surpassing power of Christ, she is liberated, doing well, and is no longer possessed.

Seven Ways Demons Harass Us

THE LOWEST LEVEL OF DEMONIC INVOLVEMENT IN OUR LIVES IS "TEMPTATION." Demons tempt everyone. God allows this for our sanctification. The next level up in their evil involvement is "harassment." Many people are subject to demonic harassment. Most of the time it is so disguised that people do not realize it is demons who are the cause.

After years of ministering to people who are victims of demonic harassment, we can identify some common types. It is important not to see a demonic cause for every negative event in life. Bad things happen to us all. But it is just as important to recognize when the Evil One is harassing us and to respond properly.

Here are seven common types of demonic harassment. No doubt, there are many more.

- **Impeding holy ministry/works.** Satan will target particularly holy works and ministries which directly interfere with his evil plans. St. Paul himself experienced this form of demonic harassment. In 1 Thes 2:18, he writes: "I decided to go to you-I, Paul, not only once but more than once-yet Satan thwarted us." Similarly, a woman in the pro-life movement shared with us a long series of inexplicable impediments to her holy work. The demons hate the pro-life movement and target it for special harassment. Another woman spoke to us of her holy work with minorities and oppressed peoples. Whenever she tried to work, she was inexplicably overcome with an intense lethargy. Deliverance prayers lifted this lethargy and thus revealed its demonic source.

- **Blocking important human connections.** In all of our lives, there are important human connections. The demons will try to manipulate, impair or block these connections. For example, a young possessed woman's relationship with her loving father was a key to her liberation. The demons regularly sent false emails, imitating either the daughter or the father, to deceive and destroy this relationship. One false text said that the father was no longer able to deal with his daughter anymore and that she should leave. It turned out, not surprisingly, that he never sent that email to her; he would never abandon her. It was purely demonic. The demons ploy was unsuccessful! Similarly, a priest exorcist tried to contact me about a difficult case for which he wanted some assistance. Both of our phones were working fine but our connection was inexplicably cut ten times in a row. It lifted after deliverance prayers were said.

- **Destroying families.** In these days, the family is one of Satan's primary targets. The demons do all sorts of deceptions to break apart the family. One of their harassments is to sow distrusting or exaggerated negative thoughts in the minds of family members. A good antidote to this is a regular family rosary. Praying together and also maintaining good communications are important in defeating Satan's sowing seeds of discord.

- **Financial distress.** The demons will target certain families, especially those who are the subject of financial curses, for ongoing financial harassment. Unexpected expenses continually crop up and/or income mysteriously disappears. Despite a solid income the family is always teetering on the edge of bankruptcy. Such situations are not the result of bad financial management but rather a continuing bizarre series of negative financial events. Some families are able to trace these difficulties to a parent or relative who intentionally cursed their finances and said, "You will never have anything."

- **Impeding Mass attendance and other sacred sacraments and prayers.** One possessed woman can never seem to get to Mass on Sunday. As she prepares to leave the house, something unexpected comes up or she suddenly starts to feel ill, and then stays home. Other people complain that they try to go to confession but a myriad of strange events hinders them from doing so. It is obvious why Satan would focus his harassment on people receiving these most efficacious holy sacraments.

- **Harassing our technology.** Demons have a special focus on obstructing technology, particularly when it is used for sacred purposes. At SMC, we regularly experience this. For example, our monthly deliverance sessions, attended by thousands, are ALWAYS harassed in different ways each month. However, we always manage to get it done. Our computers are sometimes blocked from connecting to our website and app, or apps to record our social media videos are inexplicably not functioning. I regularly receive notes from people who cannot register for our sessions or pray with our videos, even though thousands of others can do so. Some of these are normal technical glitches, but others have a preternatural cause. One of our SMC staff mentioned St. Carlo Acutis, perhaps he could help with IT. It turns out, he was a web designer. So, we started to invoke St. Carlo at the beginning of our online sessions. The first time we did so, our monthly session went off without a hitch. Perhaps he will become the patron saint of the internet and electronics. *St. Carlo Acutis, pray for us and protect our communications!*

• **Overt Harassment.** Sometimes the demons drop the disguise and overtly harass people. In exorcism sessions, they will throw crucifixes across the room. They will send harassing texts or make bogus phone calls to the afflicted, team members, family members and exorcists. They will break religious objects such as rosary beads or statues. Occasionally a possessed person or team member will call in a panic in response to such demonic antics: "The rosary was broken and the cross thrown across the room! What should I do?" My calm response, "Pick it up."

Similarly, one of our spiritual sensitives had a dish thrown across the room and smashed by demons. I had given her the dish as a gift from the Holy Land. On it was a picture of the famous mosaic of the loaves and the fishes from Tabgha. The demons were trying to make a point. I responded by buying her two more of those dishes. I told her that if the demons break these two, I will buy her four more. The demons gave up.

Also, loud bangs and other noises are sometimes heard. People are invisibly pushed down stairs or touched or scratched or bruised. Warning notes are etched on mirrors. Satanic symbols suddenly appear on the afflicted person's body. These occur and many more. With overt harassment, the demons are trying to incite fear and/or dominance. They want to distract or dissuade an exorcist or the afflicted person from continuing the exorcism or other holy actions.

With hidden or overt harassment, there is always a goal. Satan and his minions do not do "random." But it is obvious that the Evil One is chained. If he was not, he could easily control and destroy any human being or thwart any project. As Scripture tells us: Jesus is the one who overcomes the "strong man" and "takes away the armor on which he relied" (Lk 11:22). Thus, with Satan chained, we always manage to get the job done, although it takes a bit of persistence and faith. God uses this harassment to strengthen our trust and faith in Him.

In response to demonic harassment, we (1) trust in God; (2) exercise patience; (3) offer deliverance prayers. Our app and website have a number of specific prayers in response to different types of demonic harassment. More general protection and deliverance prayers are also available and very effective, although persistence and trust is needed. At times, the Evil One might seem to have the upper hand, but it is not so. Jesus is Lord and He ALWAYS wins!

The Power
of Sacramentals

SACRAMENTALS ARE A STAPLE OF EXORCISTS. Sacramentals are not one of the seven sacraments instituted by Jesus (e.g. baptism, Eucharist). Rather, they are typically religious objects which, when used in faith, confer actual graces. These objects receive their power not from an inherent spiritual force, but rather from authority given by Christ to the Church. They are not magic talismans, but rather objects, dedicated to a holy use, which invoke the power of Christ. In an exorcism, we witness their efficacy daily. Demons hate them!

One sacramental which was part of the pre-Vatican II Rite of Exorcism is the priest's stole. At one point during the old Rite of Exorcism, the priest lays his stole on the back of the energumen's neck. While this might not seem like much, the demons have threatened and begged me to remove the stole. "Take it off!" they demanded. The demons tried to bargain with me: "Take off the stole and I will answer your question." I was demanding to know their names. Of course, I did not comply. We don't bargain with demons. Rather, we invoke the power of Christ and command them to be obedient.

One of the most powerful sacramentals is a crucifix. In fact, holding up a crucifix and saying, *"Ecce crucem domini, fugite partes adversae"* (Behold the cross of the Lord, depart you evil powers) is an integral part of the Rite of Exorcism, old and new. Often when I hold the crucifix up, I command the demons to look at it and I say, "Look at the sign of your defeat." It was on the cross that the kingdom of Satan was forever smashed. The crucifixion of Jesus and his resurrection is the fundamental exorcism and the source of efficacy of all exorcisms. The demons know this and they cannot bear to look at the Truth. Many times, energumens will say, as the cross is raised up, that it hurts their eyes to look at it. In reality, it is the demons who are tormented.

Another sacramental which is a part of every exorcism is holy water. An oft-quoted comment from St. Teresa of Avila bears repeating: "From long experience I have learned that there is nothing like holy water to put devils to flight." There is no life-giving water in hell (Lk 16:22). When water is blessed by the Church, it becomes "holy" and it is incredibly tormenting to the Evil One.

Every seasoned exorcist has witnessed the power of holy water. Not uncommonly, when it is sprinkled on the possessed person in the midst of an exorcism, the person exclaims that it "burns." For some, the pain is incredibly intense, despite the fact that the water is actually lukewarm or even cold. Such an experience is a sign that the person truly has demons.

One of our afflicted persons was having problems communicating on her phone. So, we suggested she put a sticker with an image of the medal of St. Benedict and attach it to her phone. She said she put the sticker on the phone and when she tried to pick up the phone, she said it felt like it burned. She could hardly hold it. Similarly, during one of our exorcism sessions a few weeks ago, a crucifix on the wall loudly snapped and the Benedictine medal on it flew off the wall and crashed to the ground.

It is very clear that the demons hate this medal. Practitioners of magic invoke talismans and magic formulas. We do neither of these. The power of the medal does not come from an inherent power in the medal itself or some magic ritual done over it. Rather, it invokes the authority of the Church and the intercession of St. Benedict, who is the patron of exorcists. On the medal are exorcistic inscriptions including some ancient exorcistic prayers of the Church.

For many years, the meaning of the letters on the medal was lost. In 1647, a manuscript, dated 1415, was found in a monastery in Bavaria which explained the symbols. The letters around the outside of the medal are: V.R.S.N.S.M.V.—S.M.Q.L.I.V.B. *Vade Retro Satana, Nunquam Suade Mihi Vana; Sunt Mala Quae Libas, Ipse Venena Bibas. Begone Satan! Never tempt me with your vanities! What you offer me is evil. Drink the poison yourself!*

The Benedictine medal is the only sacramental I am aware of that actually includes an exorcism on it. And very clearly, it has a powerful effect on the demonic. Many in this ministry put stickers with the symbol of the Benedictine medal on their phones and computers. When using our electronic devices, we have had more than a little demonic harassment. Also, we often use a crucifix with a Benedictine medal on it during our exorcisms. We encourage our laity to use these medals as well.

It is especially helpful to find out which sacramentals are most effective in each case. It varies depending on the specific demons that are present. Knowledge of the demonic portals that allowed the demons to enter the person can be helpful. Most often, a trial-and-error approach is used. We have on hand many, many sacramentals and will see which ones provoke the strongest demonic reaction and thus appear to be most effective in that particular case.

For example, one of our afflicted young women had been struggling mightily to be rid of the demons. She was cursed by her mother, a witch, and dedicated to Satan in her womb. This is a high-level contract and one that took concerted effort to break. Before she converted to the faith, she had a very troubled history, especially sexually, including having had an abortion.

In the midst of one of the early sessions, one of the images held up was the image of Our Lady of Guadalupe. The demonic reaction was strong; clearly this image was having a powerful effect. It turns out that, in the miraculous image of Our Lady of Guadalupe, Mary is depicted as being pregnant. Of course, she is carrying Jesus the Son of God in her womb. So, she is often considered patroness of the unborn. Clearly these demons of abortion were being overcome by this holiest of women under her title of Patroness of the Unborn.

Some time later, her father bought her a religious medal depicting Our Lady of Guadalupe to wear around her neck. He had it blessed. The day before he met with her daughter to give it to her, the demons sent him a threatening text: "You're not putting that chain on her tomorrow. You won't dare …One day you [expletive deleted]." Shortly after he put it around her neck, she yelled, "Ouch!" On her leg was, inexplicably, a two-inch cut. At the very same time the cut happened, another text appeared on the father's phone cussing him out. The demons can threaten and they can cause some limited torment and hurt, but the medal is now solidly around her neck and she wears it proudly. It is interesting that, for many days after wearing the medal, the demonic assaults were much more limited. The medal "works."

Similarly, exorcists use another very effective sacramental from the saints. Exorcists often collect first class relics of the saints, which might be a little piece of bone from their tomb or hair or blood from the saint. All demons are different and have their own personalities. Thus, some saints are more effective against particular demons. Of course, some saints are always effective such as the Virgin Mary. St. Joseph, who sometimes is known as the "Terror of Demons" and much under-appreciated by many, is a staple in our sessions.

We especially ask the possessed persons if they have a devotion to a particular saint. In one recent case, the woman said she had a devotion to St. Charbel Makhlouf. We invoked a variety of saints during the opening litany of the saints. But when we mentioned St. Charbel, the reaction was immediate and strong. So, we stayed with invoking his presence for several minutes, with positive effects.

Demons cannot stand anything holy. Thus, any holy object torments them. It is remarkable and instructive just how much these holy objects torment them. They scream when coming in contact with them. Why? The answer is rather simple. They cannot stand God or anything connected to God. To be holy simply means to have some of God's presence or radiance connected to the object. From the beginning, they rejected God and now, in the darkness of hell, the light of God and His radiance causes them supreme torment.

Having witnessed the graced power of these sacramentals and their effect of casting out demons, my house is full of such sacramentals. I have a holy water font I use when I enter the house. I have pictures of the saints on my walls and crucifixes. Benedictine stickers are placed on my computers, and more. Surely everyone should make generous use of these powerful instruments of God's grace.

Generational Curses: Real or Imagined?

"JAMES" WAS A SEVERE ALCOHOLIC. After a serious illness that almost took his life, James stopped drinking. He vowed to return to his faith after having lapsed for a decade. However, when he started going back to the Catholic Mass, he began to have strange reactions.

He blacked out several times while engaging in religious practices. At night, he felt attacked by evil forces. He woke up with large bruises and scratches on his arms and legs. The scratches were in sets of threes [note: demonic scratches are often in threes as a mockery of the Trinity].

Strangely, even though he had stopped drinking, bottles of alcohol would inexplicably materialize around him. His sister actually witnessed the bottles suddenly appear at his side as if dropping from his body. Evil forces appeared to be tempting him.

His parish priest referred him to our exorcism ministry. In the initial sessions, he made great progress. In addition to attending weekly exorcism sessions, he prayed a daily rosary and frequented the sacraments, including regular confession. However, after a few weeks, he suddenly stopped going to the sessions. He stopped receiving the sacraments and said he no longer believed. It was a stunning halt with no obvious explanation.

But a few short months later, he returned. He told the Exorcist that the spiritual attacks had gotten so bad that he couldn't stand it. The exorcism sessions began again and were again having noticeable benefit. The demonic attacks were starting to get less severe.

However, it seemed to the Exorcist that there was something blocking full liberation. The sessions were not being fully effective. On an inspiration, the Exorcist asked James, "Is there any freemasonry or other cult involvement in your family background?" James responded, "My grandfather was a 33rd degree mason." [Note: On November 13, 2023, in a letter to Philippine Bishops, the CDF reaffirmed its prohibition of membership in Freemasonry because of "the irreconcilability between Catholic doctrine and Freemasonry."]

So, the Exorcist took James through the prayers from our website to lift any curses related to freemasonry plus any other generational curses. In the next session, James experienced great relief. He said it was almost like "a switch turned" and he was soon liberated. It has been several years now and the demons have not returned. He is happily married and practicing the faith.

In another case, a woman had, through no apparent fault of her own, generational evil spirits including freemasonry from the family line. She was determined to follow a religious vocation and the demons were having none of it. The battle ensued. She held up her end with valor. Much initial progress had been made, although the intensive sessions took a toll on everyone present. At one point, an attending priest took out a relic of Fr. Michael McGivney, beatified founder of the Knights of Columbus, and handed it to the Exorcist. Interestingly, Fr. McGivney originally founded the charitable Knights of Columbus partly as a Catholic alternative to the lure of the secretive, cultic Freemasons. The Exorcist took the relic and said, "Through the intercession of Blessed Fr. Michael McGivney, I command the demons to leave!" The young woman said she heard the demons mocking him, "That country priest, are you kidding me!?" Exorcists recognize in demons' mocking behavior often their underlying terror of what is to come.

Then the Exorcist said, "I ask the Lord to manifest the sanctity of Fr. Michael McGivney through the pain the demons endure." The demons let out a blood-curdling scream. More so than during the previous prayers, these screams were louder and tinged with desperation. It was clear to everyone in the room that something important was happening. The relic was then placed on the crown of the afflicted woman's head and the demons let out another blood-curdling scream. As the same time, the attending priest read the "Prayer for the Canonization of Blessed Michael McGivney." Each time the relic touched her body, she writhed and screamed.

The Exorcist again commanded the demons to leave through the intercession of Fr. McGivney. She convulsed and started to cough up a white frothy foam—typical in an exorcism especially as demons begin to leave. Then the writhing and screams stopped. The woman came back to herself and was at peace. It was clear that a number of the demons had just departed.

The exorcism had been moving forward but when Fr. McGivney was invoked, it was taken to a new level. Upon reflection, we were not surprised that Fr. McGivney was so effective against demons of freemasonry, since he had dedicated his life to a holy Catholic alternative: the Knights of Columbus. Moreover, the reactions of the demons confirmed our own conviction of the sanctity of Blessed Fr. Michael McGivney. We will certainly invoke this holy priest's intercession in future exorcisms, especially when the demons of freemasonry are involved.

There is some discussion today about whether generational spirits really exist. The Catholic Church has not spoken definitively about this and there is much room for disagreement and debate.[14] Indeed, the faithful are not required to believe or accept the existence of generational curses. However, the senior exorcists that I know all make lifting generational curses a regular part of their ministry.

Some theologians disagree and suggest that the sacrament of baptism would completely eradicate any transmission of the effects of generational sins. It is true that baptism cleanses the person from the stain of Original Sin. However, it does not wipe out all its effects. For example, suffering and death remain in our world because of Original Sin, despite the power of baptism.

Others teach that we are not culpable for the sins of past generations. This is definitely true! But the effects of their sins can and do affect us. For example, if a person's parents were both drug addicts, that person is not responsible for their sins. But the negative effects of growing up in a drug addicted household would certainly affect the child.

For individuals with a family history of freemasonry, our team has been a bit surprised at the extent of spiritual problems they experience as a result. These individuals not uncommonly have a repeating generational history of similar dysfunctions. For some, it is the presence of a spirit of death or for others it is a repeating generational experience of physical maladies or financial curses. For those inheriting a spirit of death, these families may have an abnormal generational history of suicides, homicides, early deaths, miscarriages and/ or abortions.

Freemasonry in one's family lineage is one of the most striking examples of generational curses. But there are others. We had a woman who was terribly possessed apparently as a result of her family's involvement in providing abortions. While she was not involved, earlier generations were, including actually performing abortions in the home. It took several years of intense exorcisms before she experienced much relief.

It does not seem fair that we would suffer from the sins of past generations. Indeed, it is not. But there are many ways that innocent children suffer as the result of previous generations' sins. Our experience, and the experience of other exorcists, makes a clear connection between the sins of one's past generations and demonic afflictions in the present. A family history of occult practice, witchcraft, abortions, freemasonry and other similar occult organizations all seem to have ugly repercussions down through several generations.

I have noticed that lifting generational curses seems relatively easy for most, as it was for the aforementioned cases. Perhaps it is because the children are not culpable for the sins and thus the evil passed down was not as entrenched. On the other hand, I have found that casting out the effects of divination and occult practices, such as the practice of witchcraft, if the individuals themselves had engaged in this serious sin, is not easy and takes considerable time and cleansing.

When we try to discern with a demonically afflicted person the source of the evil, we sometimes have to look at their preceding generations. It is not uncommon that we will find the source there and this helps to direct our exorcism prayers. Lifting generational spirits is currently a significant part of many, if not most, of the exorcists in the USA and some other countries such as the Philippines. As long as it appears to be helpful, exorcists will certainly continue to do so.

Our Guardian Angel Leads Us Home

IN A RECENT POLL, 69% OF AMERICANS BELIEVE IN THE EXISTENCE OF ANGELS. A full 20% believe that they have had a personal encounter with an angel or a demon.[15] More people have personal experiences of the angelic world than might be publicly apparent.

A member of our team said that he was about to go to sleep and felt a spiritual "nudge" to text a friend. He believed it came from his guardian angel. He was hesitant and not sure how the other person would react. He did so anyway and he included a promise of prayers. The friend responded immediately and was very grateful. A grandparent had just died. His friend's text and ensuing telephone conversation was a real consolation. The experience confirmed for the man the importance of listening in prayer to one's guardian angel, who ultimately is inspired by God.

The Catholic Church has long taught that each of us has a guardian angel to guide us throughout our lives on our way to God's Kingdom. In a demonic inversion of the sacred, some occultists posit that you have a *personal spirit* or a *spirit guide*. This is a typical deception of the occult—it uses similar phrases to the Church but they mean very different things. Occultists attempt to connect with this spirit guide. But without the sure protections of the faith, such guides may turn out to be demons.

One of those with whom we were praying was afflicted by demons and just beginning the long process of liberation. She was visited by a spirit who claimed to be her guardian angel. Listening to what the angel was saying, she became suspicious and asked, "Does Jesus love me?" With a look of anger and hatred, the spirit snarled, "No!" She knew it was not her good guardian.

Because of such common demonic ruses during exorcisms, we always advise those afflicted with demons to ignore extraordinary spiritual experiences and to assume they are demonic until after liberation. Even then, we advise caution and consulting with a trained spiritual director.

Some have told me that they feel confident that they are personally able to discern the difference between a good spirit and a bad spirit through their own feelings during the experience. This can be a bit of spiritual hubris. As the Scriptures tell us, Satan disguises himself as an angel of light (2 Cor 11:14). I have had many people who are convinced that they are receiving special locutions from God, or visions of angels or even the BVM, but were deceived. This can even happen to those who are truly specially gifted.

For example, one gifted person has a *bona fide* charism of regularly seeing her guardian angel. She related an experience she had:

> *Late at night, my guardian angel, or at least something that looked exactly like him, appeared in my room. It was odd because previously he had never woken me up at night. But in my eyes it looked exactly like him so I continued to trust him. I found myself being*

misled. This "angel" began asking me questions about trust in God. Did I truly have trust in Him? He was saying things like: "If God truly loved you, He would have taken away these torments long ago, what kind of "Savior" is that?" This "angel" also tried to tempt me to stay away from my spiritual director, claiming that if I left and directed myself, I would have been in better shape than if I remained under him. In hindsight I should have been more careful and cautious in my discernment of spirits. Changes were made, with the help of my director, immediately after realizing that this was not of God. Now, everything that I was "seeing" was passed by him first; I no longer discerned things by myself.

Summoning "angels" in occult practices will inevitably lead to disaster. Demons are able to appear to be good spirits and deceive practitioners into thinking they are doing good and invoking good powers. However, this should not stop followers of Jesus from developing a relationship with their own spiritual guide— our good angels.

How to listen to our real guardian angel? The noise of the world can drown out their voice. We hear them best when we *pray alone* and do so in *silence.* I find it helpful to pray in front of the Lord in the Church's tabernacle, although our guardian spirit is always with us. When the good angel speaks to us, it is a voice full of God's peace. But, even then, we need to be cautious and discern the spirits.

How do we communicate with our guardian angel? Normally, angels cannot read our thoughts. But, I have been given to understand that our guardian angel has a special charism from God. When we direct our thoughts to our guardian angels, they can hear us.

I was touched by this story from a gifted person who has the special grace of seeing her guardian angel. I share it with you:

I was on my way to a place that was in a remote, hidden spot in the woods. I had never been there before. I turned off the main highway. Literally as soon as I got on this new road, I lost the signal with my phone. I had no clue of which road I was supposed take. I had been using the phone's GPS to find the center. I had no maps or any clue where the place was. I had no sense of direction, nor was I prepared to navigate through the mountains so late in the evening.

I was close to having a full-blown panic attack from being in the dark, no cell phone service, and no idea where I was going. Looking back on the situation, I should have adequately prepared and printed out a map so I would be sure of where I was going.

On the edge of tears, I cried out to my guardian angel asking for help. At the time, I did not see him in the car or next to me. Then, he appeared in the car in the passenger seat beside me. He immediately instructed me to trust. He left the inside of my car and went out in front of the car. He told me to follow him. I did.

My angel flew in front of the car about ten feet. He was hovering about two to three feet off the ground. He canted forward about 45 degrees, wings partly outstretched, and he started flying in front of me. I followed him.

In complete trust, I followed my angel through the dark, curvy, and narrow roads of the mountains. I had no clue where I was going. First, we turned off the highway and then we turned right onto a road. From there, we turned right again onto a small, narrow road. Then we took a sharp right and then we took another left that led down a backroad. Then we took another left. After about fifteen minutes in the dark, I saw the place in front of me. But there were five buildings and I didn't know which one was the right one. I stopped car and got out. When I got out of the car, my angel was still there. I was stressed. It was late at night and he led me to one of the main buildings to where the gathering was being held and then he left.

I was so relieved! I was happy, and grateful.

I love this experience because it is a perfect metaphor for our guardian angel's place in each of our lives. We are often spiritually blind, lost, and in the dark. While most of us do not have such a gift as seeing our guardian angel, if we but trust our angel, whose grace comes directly from God, our angel will lead us safely home.

My Life as an Exorcist

PEOPLE OFTEN ASK ME WHAT LIFE IS LIKE AS AN EXORCIST. I have a few thoughts...

When I started in this ministry years ago, it was a little-known, secretive ministry and I kept it quiet. Some priests in the Archdiocese didn't even know we had an exorcist. But these days, the ministry has pretty much gone out in the open. Previously, it was known among priests as a ministry that was a little odd and tended to attract odd characters. I suppose it still does!

Now that it is out in the open, some priests, especially young ones, look up to me and others think I am a little nuts. Some priests do not believe in demons including some of my friends. It has strained our relationships. One religious order rejected us. A parish disinvited us. And one priest superior won't talk to me.

If you get involved in this ministry only sporadically, the spiritual effect on oneself is limited. Satan doesn't pay you much mind and your exposure to the dark world is limited. However, if you get involved full time and handle a lot of tough cases, including lifting witches' curses, then there is a big bull's eye on your back. Witches curse you. Demons attack you. Satan threatens to kill you. And while the parishes and public may be fascinated by your ministry, most don't want you nearby. NIMBY, "not in my backyard," is more than applicable here.

I have, indeed, gone into this ministry full bore with lots of tough cases and many thousands of demons have been cast out and innumerable witches' curses lifted. Witches are mad at me and the demons hate me. This is not all bad.

More than a few priests are hesitant to enter this ministry or to get involved. They don't want to upset Satan and be a target. They don't want to have parishioners hear the possessed yelling and vomiting. They don't want crazy people hanging around. Who can blame them?

On the other side, it has had a profound effect on me and my spiritual life. Being involved with low-level demons and easier cases is not bad. But once you hit the big time and get someone who is infested with hundreds of demons and headed by one of Satan's lieutenants, the intensity ramps way up.

The Evil One will play his "A" game and you need to be more vigilant. What happens in a session is secondary to all the levels of manipulation played by the Father of Lies and Deceptions. He is a master at it and will play you like a puppet if you are not careful. You will wake up one day and realize that in a possession case in which you thought you were doing fine, you are actually getting played and losing big time. This has happened to us more than once.

So the ministry has affected me profoundly. First, *I have had to "up" my spiritual life*. I go to confession weekly without missing. I never miss saying daily Mass, even when traveling. I pray almost 2 to 3 hours a day in front of the tabernacle and I scrupulously avoid the least sin, if I can. The Evil One knows your weaknesses and he will exploit them big time.

Second, and most importantly, *I have had to radically place my trust in Jesus*. My mantra is: *Jesus I trust in you*. I must do that each moment and with each case. The demons always begin with: "She/he is mine! I won't leave. Your prayers are worthless." And so forth. In the first weeks and months of a tough case, it does appear that Satan has a powerful hold and will never leave. The possessed person moans and says it'll never work. They teeter on despair. They feel hopeless. The Team may look a bit discouraged. My response to both: Trust in Jesus! Jesus is Lord! Eventually the demons do leave.

Third, being an exorcist is not a passive role in which I look at the possessed from a distance. I have found that *the Exorcist actually journeys with the possessed person* through the darkness. We walk together. I experience a bit of what they experience. My shoes are mired in the same demonic mud and we both are enveloped in the same darkness. It is painful and hard going. So I need to be careful with who I am willing to perform an exorcism.

An exorcism is not a right. Catholics do not have a right to an exorcism. They have a right to the sacraments and access to the Church. These are the normal instruments of liberation. If I take on the wrong people for an exorcism, they could do me harm as a priest and cripple my health, with likely no improvement for them. With each person I accept, there is a strong personal commitment to walk with them, not abandon them, and to experience a bit of the darkness, pain, and the pure evil of their demons. God have mercy on us both!

Fourth, I get attacked and slimed by the demons. I mentioned earlier that an exorcism is a knife fight. You are in close to the enemy and the weapons are those of hand-to-hand combat. You see the enemies' eyes and he sees you. You are in close so you feel the evil presence. His ugly visage and evil pours out and slimes you. As previously noted, as my hand-to-hand combat instructor said in the military, "In a knife fight, you will get cut." I do get cut.

In my younger years, I might do three sessions or more in a day. Now, if I do that, I'll spend some time lying down afterwards, trying to recover. We say the cleansing prayers at the end of each session but it doesn't completely stop the slime and the draining fatigue.

Some have said that if you are in a state of grace, these things won't affect you. It is true that being in a state of grace is critical and it blocks major demonic attacks and infestation. But some get through. It's part of the job.

At night especially, the demons attack. During the sessions, at times, the demons will threaten me: "We are going to get you tonight!" Actually this is one of the few times they tell the truth. Every time they tell me they will attack me, they do. But Jesus and his beautiful Mother and the angels defend me.

Fifth, *the ministry strengthens my faith.* As I have said elsewhere, we experience all the truths of the faith in our exorcisms. We experience the power of the Church, the sacraments, the priesthood, the Bible, and sacramentals. We experience the communion of the saints, the ministry of the angels, and the overwhelming beauty and power of the Mother of God. All this and more.

People from other faiths come to us, Catholic priests, asking for an exorcism. They said they need us to cast out the demons. Many do convert to the faith when they experience it. I have found that everything the Catholic

Church teaches is true, even those uncomfortable truths which modernity likes to reject—including the reality of hell and it being well populated.

There are many, many more graces with being an exorcist. It profoundly changes you. The air we breathe is the air of the angels. I feel like I have one foot in the Kingdom. The angels surround me. The saints are my friends. I rejoice in a communion with the holy ones. My life is there, and not here. I don't think anyone can be fully involved in this ministry for years and then go back to normal parish duties. Maybe it is possible. It is probably like the difficulty that soldiers have after having been directly in combat for an extended time and then trying to reintegrate into normal, daily life.

I am grateful for this ministry. May God give me the grace and protection to do so for a few more years. But there is a limit. Eventually, even Jesus died and rose.

The Mystery of Evil

I CONTINUE TO BE STUNNED AT THE BEHAVIOR OF DE-
MONS. During an exorcism, they scream and scream and
scream but do not leave until finally forced at the end.
For them, an exorcism can best be described as pouring
boiling oil over them and lighting it. I am impressed by
their ability to withstand pain, no doubt acquired from
eons of suffering in hell. But why do it?

Apparently, Lucifer himself believes he is forced to
be locked into the spiritual battle. Some time ago during
a most difficult case, Lucifer himself was personally
present, which is VERY unusual. There are often proxies
who claim to be Lucifer but they are not. When the King
of Hell himself is present, he is surrounded by his Satanic court and flanked by many of the notable Princes
of Hell.

In the midst of this case, I commanded Lucifer himself to manifest and to be out front. Previously Beelzebul, his sycophant lieutenant, was doing the talking.
I said to Lucifer, "Why do you not leave? Why don't
you just give up?" Lucifer responded, "The same reason you do not." I took this to mean he believes he is
compelled to be locked into combat with God and the
forces of good, just as he suggested I would never give
up as well. (Although I do not feel compelled to engage
in the spiritual combat; I do so willingly in service to the
Lord. I will stop when the Lord says to do so.) Lucifer is
indeed eternally committed to rage against God.

But with each passing moment that Lucifer wars against God, the weight of his sins and ultimate punishment increases. As the ancient Rite of Exorcism tells them, "The longer you delay, the deeper your punishment." God, in His justice, will punish them not only for their original disobedience in rejecting Him, but also for each moment they torment a human being and every evil they commit. Thus, at the final judgment, their eternal torment will be much worse than the present. They know this, yet they persist.

One young priest emailed me and protested. He said that this can't be true. It is not rational that someone would know the tortuous ramifications of an evil decision and still do it. I tried to explain to him that evil is indeed irrational; I agreed with him. But it is true—demons nonetheless chose it. The demons threw off the loving freedom of obeying God for the slavish obedience to the supreme sadistic narcissist—Satan. They threw off the joys and peace of God's kingdom for an eternity of torment. They were given an infused full knowledge of the ugly ramifications of their rejection of God, yet they persisted. And they still do.

Each demon is a different being with a different personality. However, as an exorcist, I notice that all are similar in being consumed by rage, hatred and desire for revenge. This is what unites them. Their every action is meant to deceive and to destroy. But the one who is most destroyed by their actions is themselves. Evil, by its very nature, is self-defeating and self-injurious.

While human beings are not given a complete infused knowledge of the ramifications of our decisions as the angels were, we should be learning by experience. We should be learning that the "wages of sin is death"

(Rm 6:23) and that only in God do we find true joy and peace. But like the demons, many humans are likewise locked into a compulsive death spiral. Many humans, by their own choices, are committed to evil and thus committed to their own destruction. This is the mystery of evil.

I feel a great sadness when I contemplate it. I do what I can to announce the Good News, especially on our social media accounts which reaches many, especially the young. I pray that the grace of God would touch each of them, especially those immersed in evil. I have witnessed some particularly fortunate people whom the grace of God has touched and snapped them out of witchcraft or other darkness. Some will be recounted in case studies at the end of this book. I pray that there will be many, many more.

> *"For the wages of sin is death,*
> *but the gift of God is eternal life*
> *in Christ Jesus our Lord."*
> (Rm 6:23)

Satan Exploits Our Wounds

SOME CASES ARE PARTICULARLY DIFFICULT. One of the major reasons is that the person's inner wounds have not yet been healed. Someone might ask, "What difference does that make? The demons are cast out and that is the end of it!" Actually, it is not. The demons do indeed need to be cast out but the only way they will stay out is if the portals to the demonic have been closed and the person's underlying wounds are largely healed.

What is little realized is that Satan exploits the inner wounds of a person and then uses them as a portal. He sets his "hooks" in the wounds and is not definitively cast out until some significant inner healing has taken place. As noted by a demonologist: "The scourge of the occult calls out to wounded souls and feeds on their brokenness."[16]

Some of those who come for an exorcism don't believe in psychology. But psychology is literally the study of the psyche or mind. And the minds of most of the possessed need healing. It is VERY common that there would be some serious underlying wounds and/or unhealed traumas in their backgrounds. As one former occult member noted, "There were an awful lot of wounded Christians in the occultic groups she frequented."[17]

If significant healing is still needed, then the probability of full liberation is remote. The person can certainly make great progress and live a more normal life, but some of the symptoms will remain. For example, a woman who suffered serious abuse as a minor and now has a full blown Borderline Personality Disorder can indeed profit from deliverance prayers if she has a demonic affliction. The power of the demons in her life can be greatly attenuated, but the disorder itself will likely persist without healing, and she will likely suffer lesser demonic afflictions in its wake. While her borderline personality disorder will not typically be completely eradicated in therapy, it can be lessened and its influence decreased. This will likely be enough for the demonic to lose its hold.

There are, however, inner wounds which manifest as a psychological disturbance but they are not. These are really "faux" psychological disorders and stem mostly from the demonic presence. I know a woman who had such a borderline diagnosis complete with self-injurious behaviors and emotional lability. But after a couple of years of exorcisms at the hands of an excellent Italian exorcist, the demons were cast out and so was her "borderline personality." In reality, the symptoms were of a demonic origin and ceased when the demons left.

It is unhelpful and harmful when we dismiss the reality of demons and Satan's presence in this world. It is also unhelpful and harmful when we ascribe too much to demons. These minions of Satan like to take credit for every evil that we experience, but this is part of their own grandiosity and deceit.

How to find some healing? Of course, Christ himself is the ultimate healer and as we move closer to Him and He graces us in our spirit, we naturally experience healing in our psyche as well. We are not two beings: one spiritual and one psychological. Rather, we are one person uniting the spiritual and the psyche. So, when something affects us through the psyche or the spiritual, it affects the other side of us as well.

There are natural healing methods which are well known. At our center, we know some excellent Catholic psychiatrists, psychologists and social workers. They work in harmony with our spiritual deliverance efforts which combine to form a powerful healing regimen. Moreover, natural healthy healing for the body is always important such as physical exercise, a healthy diet, rest, and relaxation exercises.

Similarly, engaging in healing community activities and interpersonal relationships are very healing. We find that those who are demonically afflicted are often isolated. They do not have supportive interpersonal relationships. They have no healthy friendships. Joining a church group or volunteering in church activities can be a way of healing oneself as one is helping others. As previously noted, Satan's minions try to isolate and then systematically torment and destroy. Holy friends are a support both spiritually as well as psychologically.

Of course, we steer clear of New Age "healing" such as reiki, shamans, healing witches, curanderas and the like. While they say they are healing people, the source of their power does not come from God and thus cannot truly heal. They can effect a short-term alleviation of some symptoms, but often the symptoms later return with even greater intensity.

More than a few people are pounding at the door of our center and desperately seeking an exorcism. Some of them do need the ministry of an exorcist and the solemn Rite of Exorcism and we do our best to provide such. But the vast majority are not fully possessed and do not need the full Rite. The normal means of liberation from Satan's grasp is living a healthy and holy life including regular reception of the Sacraments including confession and Eucharist, fervent daily prayers, and other pious practices such as daily rosary and Eucharistic adoration. I would add natural holy physical and psychological healing and support.

True and lasting liberation takes time and one's patience is sorely tried when tormented by the Evil One. We offer our sufferings in union with the Passion of the Christ and pray that our little sufferings contribute, in union with Christ, to our own healing and sanctification, and the sanctification of our families and our world.

Victim Souls

"M" WAS POSSESSED. We eventually became convinced that she was a true victim soul, i.e., she became possessed not because she did anything wrong or was wronged by someone else, such as being cursed. Rather, we believe God allowed her to be possessed as a kind of spiritual crucifixion for the salvation of other souls.

These cases are VERY rare. Too often exorcists will diagnose such a victim case of possession because they could not find a demonic opening. But they are usually not correct. It would be important to look for signs of sanctity in the possessed victim soul. Moreover, such victim souls typically go on to live a specially graced, mystical life.

As a true victim soul, M would be a high-profile case. Satan would know something of spiritual importance was up and he would marshal his strongest forces against her. And he did. M was possessed by hundreds of demons, as the demons were forced to admit. The list of the leading demons present sounded like a "Who's Who" in hell such as Baal, Beelzebul, Leviathan, and more. Lucifer himself was personally present and led the entire demonic colony. One of those high-ranking demons would make it an ugly case; we had the demonic "All Star" team.

The exorcism took intense weekly sessions for two years. Sadly, M was emotionally raped repeatedly by the demons. She was levitated—the demons picked her up and threw her against the wall. She was tortured, burned, clawed and pummeled. She lost a lot of weight and we became concerned about her health. In response, she tried to keep down some food although she vomited several times a day. This stopped when we had her take tablespoons of blessed oil.

The entire process of the exorcism took the team and myself to the limit. She, too, was pressed to her limits. She had suicidal thoughts and her health was slipping. We monitored her closely. But I knew that time was not on our side. We could not stand much more. We had to finish this quickly.

It had been over a year of intense sessions and not one demon had left. The Team was losing hope. Some suggested we should refer her elsewhere such as the exorcism team in a nearby diocese. We were losing hope that we would ever succeed. But I knew that if we were not successful, there was no reason why they would be. We were doing what the Church had done for centuries.

One afternoon, we were about to finish another session. The demons had been screaming for two hours, as they did during every session. But none left. I was about to finish the session anyway, but I said to the demonic leader, "If one demon leaves, we will end the session." The response was: "Ok." One demon left.

This might have been ill-advised and perhaps it could have been considered making a "deal" with the demons (I was going to finish the session anyway). But one demon did leave. It didn't sound like much in light of almost 1,000 demons being present. But, at that moment, I knew that we had them. We were going to win. If one demon could be cast out, then it was only time before they all left.

Our morale shifted. Lucifer miscalculated. They don't worry about "morale" in hell. Later, Lucifer admitted tangentially that he had made a mistake and had not considered the impact on our morale. And it must have rattled the rest of the demons present as well. They, too, had to admit that they were vulnerable.

Now, the countdown was on. Session after session more demons were cast out until finally only Lucifer remained. And finally, the Virgin Mother herself showed up and cast him out, as is fitting.

It is often said that God does not allow us to be tempted or tried beyond our abilities to hold up. We were pressed to the limit. Most importantly, our heartfelt admiration for the young female victim soul who endured all of this for the Kingdom. She has since gone on to a hidden, mystical life.

There have been others who have been thought to be possessed by demons as victim souls. Most notably, it is said by some (although some sources disagree) that St. Mary of Jesus Crucified, i.e. the "little Arab," was such a soul. She had many mystical gifts, as is common with real victim souls, including ecstasies, visions of Our Lady, and the stigmata. As a sign of her extraordinary sanctity, she called herself God's "little nothing." This penetrating humility is a true sign of sanctity.

It is said that Satan was granted a special time of 40 days, much like Job, to tempt and torture St. Mary of Jesus Crucified. He did so mercilessly. During it all, the Little Arab prayed, "I unite myself to Jesus and Mary. I offer my suffering for those who are against the Church. Blessed be my God!" Satan was forced to admit, "The three most powerful things against us are charity, humility, and obedience." Satan was also forced to admit,

"She walks in the footsteps of the Master and that is why she is strong."[18] The Servant of God Marie de Vallees, 17th century mystic and directee of St. John Eudes, was also thought to have undergone a period of demonic possession as a victim soul. So, too, Blessed Eustochium of Padua.

Almost all great saints and mystics were attacked and pummeled by demons: Padre Pio, Catherine of Siena, Gemma Galgani, and many many more. Were they actually possessed? Or simply externally attacked by Satan? All endured much at the hands of demons although it is debated whether some were actually possessed. Those nearby and the saints themselves often thought they were possessed and asked for an exorcism. The great majority were not. But with great graces come great sufferings. Sufferings at the hands of demons go with the territory of being a great saint. Ironically, Satan's every action of hatred and violence against such holy souls only leads to their sanctification and great graces for many others.

These experiences also make an important point: being possessed does not mean one is damned. Once a team member told a possessed person that she should get freed as soon as possible so she doesn't go to hell when she dies. This is wrong and I corrected her. Satan can only control the body and he can have strong influence on the mind. But he cannot control the will and the soul of the person.

In fact, it is the inner free will of the person that rejects Satan and wants to be freed which is a critical key to an exorcism. With souls that do not want to be freed but actually welcome the demons, the state is called "perfect possession." For them, an exorcism is not possible. The soul must reject Satan and fight alongside the Exorcist to come to freedom in Christ.

I am also convinced that many of those who are possessed and fight with the Exorcist to find freedom in Christ actually can become holy souls. While I do not wish the state of possession on anyone, those who are possessed and go through the painful trial of being freed by Christ are thus purified in a very intense and extraordinary way. While they might not be like the great saints in virtue, their steadfast faith and patient endurance surely brings them to a real sense of sanctity. It is not surprising that almost all of our former clients who found freedom from possession are now in the front pews of their church. Christ turned their suffering into grace, as only He can do.

But, back to the original question: are there souls who are temporarily possessed by Satan as purely victim souls? Many reject the notion, but I am convinced it does happen. I firmly believe I experienced it with one possessed person. I am confident I won't experience it again. It is very, very rare. Regardless of what one believes about the possibility of victim possession, all the great saints and holy mystics were attacked by the Evil One and subject to great temptations and physical attacks.

Regardless of whether the demons were externally attacking the saints or actually possessing their bodies, they suffered greatly and by their offering of their sufferings for others, they became a source of great graces for others and for the world. We ought to imitate them and likewise offer to God our little sufferings for ourselves and for the world.

Mistakes Exorcists Make

BEING AN EXORCIST IS VERY SAFE. Some are frightened and do not undertake this ministry because of this fear. This can be a lack of faith. Trust in Jesus! He is Lord. Satan is terrified of Him and Satan is also afraid of the exorcist. As the famous exorcist Fr. Gabriel Amorth said: "Satan is afraid of me!"

Being an exorcist is a bit like being a pilot in that both are very safe….but they are not kind to major mistakes. I have made some mistakes learning to be an exorcist, and I still do. Fortunately, none were huge mistakes and God has had mercy upon me. But I do know of a number of exorcists who have made serious mistakes, some even destroying their ability to minister as a priest. I list a few of the common mistakes of exorcists:

1. Forgetting Christ is the Exorcist.

Demons try to goad the Exorcist into a one-on-one fight. Similarly, listening to the demons scream in an exorcism, the Exorcist can be filled with a sense of his own "power." He then forgets that it is really Christ who is the exorcist. Thus, he is filled with spiritual arrogance. Demons make mincemeat of a priest who thinks he can beat the demons by himself. Whenever the demons tempt me: "Oh, you are so powerful" or some such, I say: "No, it is Jesus who casts you out."

Exorcists can err on the other extreme and believe that their ministry is ineffective and just not working. The demons will taunt the exorcist and tell him that he has no power over them. They will tell him what a sinner he is and fill his mind with doubts and thoughts denigrating his self-image. This, too, is a temptation. The Exorcist should remind himself that the power to cast out demons does not come from himself. Rather, Christ gave the Church the authority to cast out demons and the Bishop has delegated this power to him. The power to cast out demons thus comes from Christ. The Exorcist is just Our Lord's poor instrument. As a line in the old Rite of Exorcism says, "I adjure you not by my weakness but by the might of the Holy Spirit to depart from this servant of God."

2. Losing Control of the Exorcism Session.

Demons do everything they can to derail an exorcism. The prayers cause them excruciating pain and they do everything they can to hang on and not to be cast out. As such, they will distract the Exorcist with useless chatter. They will scream and utter distracting statements and threats. They will throw things across the room. They will encourage conflicts and divisions in the Team. They will even levitate the possessed person. All these are merely attempts to derail the session. I am not a control-freak but in an exorcism, I need to stay in charge. As I tell new exorcists in training: "If you don't control the exorcism session, the demons will."

3. Confusing Mental Illness with Possession.

This is a very common mistake made by new exorcists. It is common for those suffering from psychosis to think they have demons. The mentally ill sometimes hear ugly, blasphemous, evil thoughts in their brains and assume it is demons. They feel internally tortured. They will even "manifest" when prayed over, sometimes yelling or writhing in response.

However, a seasoned exorcist who has some spiritual sensitivities can sense that no demons are present. In these cases, the Exorcist does not sense the presence of pure evil. Moreover, the yelling and "manifestations" during the session sound and feel all-too-human.

From time to time, I will sprinkle unblessed tap water on the person and/or recite some innocuous Latin sentences. Those who are not possessed, but are convinced they are, will sometimes do their best imitation of a possessed person that they have seen in the movies. When this happens, I gently shut down the session and recommend an on-going prayer regimen which would well serve any pious Catholic. But I will not continue with exorcisms.

If the Exorcist does not distinguish between mental illness and demonic possession, he is likely to spend A LOT of time, even years, praying over seriously mentally ill people with limited or no real progress. Often such people will INSIST on more prayers and more sessions. In the process, the limited resources of the Exorcist and the Team are taken up in a useless, and perhaps even counterproductive, effort.

One might speculate that it might even be one of Satan's ruses: having the Exorcist exhaust himself and the Team in such a useless pursuit. Indeed, one of Satan's attacks on the Exorcist is to push him into a state of burnout. This ministry is spiritually exhausting and requires a prudent allocation of time and limited resources. There are increasing number of people who are insisting they are possessed and demanding the personal attention of the exorcist priest and the Team. The Exorcist must discern which individuals he can and should assist. Those suffering from major mental illnesses are rarely fully possessed, despite their seeming demonic symptoms.

4. Crossing Boundaries with the Possessed.

An exorcist typically has a somewhat intense relationship with the possessed person. They meet regularly for months perhaps years. He becomes familiar with very personal details of the person's life. The possessed are often young women from abusive backgrounds. They are usually frightened, vulnerable, and needy. It is only natural that they would want to cling to the person of the Exorcist. This is a recipe for disaster.

In recent years, there have been at least a couple exorcists who have become sexually involved with the possessed. These cases are well known and adjudicated. There are even more cases where the relationship, while not being physically acted out, has become a bit enmeshed and unhealthy. It is true that if an exorcist has an unhealthy, excessively close relationship with a possessed person, even if it is not physically acted out, he may end up with some demons clinging to him. The demons can use such an unhealthy relationship as a portal to worming their way into the Exorcist's life. And one of the highest priorities for demons in the case of a possessed person is to destroy the priest's vocation. This will not only stop this exorcism but all the others he is doing.

Our exorcism team has pretty much solved this potential problem. Afflicted females interact with lay women team members exclusively, except for the exorcism sessions themselves. And in every exorcism, there are several team members present including women if the client is a woman. As an exorcist, I am never alone with the afflicted person. If that person needs to go to confession or spiritual direction, they work with their pastors or directors. This has worked well as a protection for the afflicted and for the Exorcists.

5. Being Misled by False Sensitives & Spiritual Experiences.

One of Satan's common tricks is misleading the Exorcist with false spiritual experiences.

For example, as noted previously, it is common that a possessed person will report mystical experiences with the Virgin Mary or special spiritual gifts such as mystical knowledge, locutions or prophecies. We always tell the possessed that if they have a mystical experience during the long process of liberation, they should assume it is from the Evil One. We remind them that Satan can disguise himself as an angel of light and often does!

Also, exorcists often have spiritually gifted people helping them with their ministry. Typically, people who claim to have great spiritual gifts will present themselves to exorcists and want to help. Many of them are deluded either by a false spirit or by their own imaginings. Exorcists who have relied on them have more than a few times been misled, with potentially dangerous results. The Scriptures are clear: "Test the spirits to see whether they belong to God" (1 Jn 4:1).

Similarly, exorcists themselves are often tempted to think they have special gifts or special mystical insights. While it is certainly possible for the priest to receive such graces, they are just as likely to come from the Evil One. Some exorcists become puffed up with spiritual pride believing that they are special spiritual people, plus some people these days put exorcists on a spiritual pedestal. It is noteworthy that Fr. Gabriel Amorth, the famous Roman exorcist, saw himself simply as a priest with a ministry to cast out demons. He did so faithfully and humbly for many years until his passing.

Being an exorcist is a wonderful, grace-filled ministry. Canon 1172 recommends to the Bishop that an exorcist be a priest of "piety, knowledge, prudence and integrity of life." A priest struggling with addictions, mood disorders, scrupulosity, chastity or other such difficulties would not be appropriate. Moreover, exorcists typically are older priests who have weathered decades of ministry and hopefully cast out some of their own "demons." If a young priest is called to be an exorcist, I would strongly recommend he work under the supervision of a senior exorcist.

We have lost a few of our good priests to mistakes made in combating the Evil One. I pray we do not lose any more and I hope the ministry of St. Michael Center for Spiritual Renewal assists them in ministering with integrity and faith. As I say to new exorcists: Follow the rules! Stay in the boat (of the Catholic Church)! Trust in Jesus!

The Power of the Keys: Grace vs. Magic

SOME TIME AGO, AT THE BEGINNING OF THE FORMAL RITE OF EXORCISM, I PRAYED OUT LOUD IN A FIRM VOICE: "I INVOKE THE FULL AUTHORITY OF THE KEYS OF ST. PETER AND I COMMAND THE DEMONS TO LEAVE!" The reaction was immediate and intense. The demons jerked back in agony and terror. Clearly, the demons recognized the Church's authority and were reeling at the mention of it.

Some afflicted people come to an exorcism expecting the priest to read arcane, mysterious prayers that have a kind of magical power. But if you read the Rite of Exorcism with those magical expectations, you will likely be disappointed. The Rite is simply a series of prayers, albeit of ancient origin refined and tested over hundreds of years, which are full of Scriptural references, invoking the power of God in Jesus to cast out the demons.

For example, the imperative prayer in the new Rite includes the following:

> I command you, Satan, prince of this world: acknowledge the power and strength of Jesus Christ, who defeated you in the desert, overcame you in the garden, despoiled you on the Cross, and, rising from the tomb, transferred your spoils into the kingdom of light.

The Scriptural references in the above passage are obvious. Experience in exorcisms shows that Satan has a particular abhorrence in recognizing how Christ overcame him. He does not like to be reminded of his defeats!

There is no great mystery to the prayers in the Rite of Exorcism or their meaning. To believe there are special prayers with a hidden, secret power is to fall prey to a mentality of magic and not grace. Magic is what witches and sorcerers profess to practice. We Christians rely on God and His grace.

To miss the power of the Church's prayers over the Prince of Darkness would be to miss the source of their true efficacy. The power does not come from some magical incantation. Rather, Jesus Christ, truly human and Divine, has conquered the Evil One and has given to the Church his power to cast out demons.

I regularly remind new exorcists in training: do not search for some special prayer that will magically cast out the demons. The great weapon against Satan, which is the weapon given to you, is the power of Christ in his Church. The core of an exorcism is the Church's formal Rite wielded by a priest given the proper authority from the Bishop. Never doubt it!

This is why I insist that our exorcists, in conducting a session, always include saying the Church's Rite of Exorcism at least once all the way through during each session. The demons may be howling at the mention of a particular saint and may have a complete meltdown when encountering a particular sacramental such as holy water or a relic. And we would indeed stick with that sacramental for some extra time since it seems to be most efficacious. However, I insist we include praying the full Rite, even if the demons seem not to react to it at all.

The demons can fake a reaction to something of minor effect and hide their reaction to what really is effective. I have witnessed them doing so. Thus, the Exorcist should not take the amount of demonic howling as his only barometer of what is effective in a session. Rather, we rely on our basic theology: what is ultimately effective in an exorcism is an ordained priest with faculties from the Bishop saying the official prayers of the Church, i.e., the Rite of Exorcism. Christ has given the authority to cast out demons to his Church and we exercise that authority.

Almost daily I receive requests from people asking for a special prayer that will magically give a desired result. While there are prayers for specific intentions, what is essential in all prayer is opening one's heart to God and presenting heartfelt petitions. This is what I typically recommend: no need to search for a special prayer. Rather, open your heart to God and tell Him what you need. A heartfelt prayer from a beloved Son or Daughter, which we all are, is a most efficacious prayer.

And if the Church has given us special prayers then, of course, they should be used. Thus, we pray the "Our Father," as Jesus asked us. We pray the "Hail Mary" and the rosary, a prayer loved by the Mother of Jesus and encouraged by the Church. The Liturgy of the Hours has a special efficacy as official prayers of the Church. And there are others. But what is common to all is that we open our hearts to God and we invoke the infinite power of Christ in his Church.

Sometimes I hear New Agers speak of invoking special human powers or some vague force in the universe.

One young woman claimed she had the power to control demons which she presumably exercised in her practice of magic. This is a VERY spiritually dangerous notion and likely the demons are playing her. A common element to all New Age practices is the belief in some innate human power and the belief that the human person is the center of the universe. This is perhaps the greatest error of all these alternative "spiritualities." As a Christian, we recognize that God is the center of all creation and that all power is His.

Some time ago, I was speaking with a young person and I was encouraging him to go to Church. He said, "Why? I am a good person." He added that he was confident he would go to heaven because he was good. In an exorcism, it is very clear that we humans have no intrinsic power to cast out demons and we certainly cannot save ourselves. They do not respond to reason, appeals to kindness, or any other positive motive. Only a power greater than Satan can force him out.

As noted previously, an essential and iconic part of every exorcism is the priest holding up a crucifix and saying, "*Ecce crucem Domini. Fugite partes adversae*" (Behold the cross of the Lord; depart you evil powers.) When forced to look at the cross in a well-known exorcism, the demons responded, "I cannot bear it. Oh, this is torture! It is unbearable!"[19]

What the young man does not realize is that the power to rescue us from Satan's clutches only comes through Jesus. He alone can save us (Acts 4:12). In the Sacrament of Baptism, the priest similarly holds up a crucifix and prays, "I claim you for Christ our Savior by the sign of his cross." Satan's hold over us is smashed on the cross and this salvation is present to us in baptism and the sacraments. Jesus' power to save comes to us through his Church. As he said to his disciples: "Whoever listens to you, listens to me" (Lk 10:16).

Don't believe it? Attend an exorcism and watch what happens to the devil when the power of Christ in the Church is invoked. In an exorcism last week, I commanded the demons to answer the question: "Did she receive Jesus in the Eucharist this morning? Can you feel the presence of Christ in her?" Cover your ears because the demons will start to scream!

I have come to experience more and more fully that I, as a human being, have no intrinsic power of my own. When I walk into an exorcism, I am aware of how weak and frail I am. The smallest demon could overcome me in seconds. But there is a true power in the universe and one upon which I rely. This truly infinite power is totally reliable and has never failed me. Jesus is the "strong man" of Scripture who has bound the Evil One and destroyed his Kingdom (Lk 11:21-22).

A Taste of Hell
and
A Taste of Heaven

STEPPING INTO AN EXORCISM, THE EXORCIST, TEAM AND THE POSSESSED ENTER AND ENCOUNTER THE WORLD OF THE DEMONIC. We taste a bit of what hell is like. And it is incredibly nasty. When demons speak, they criticize, belittle, and taunt; they spew hatred and violence. The look of evil and rage in their eyes is a taste of hell. Sometimes when I try to predict what the demons will do next in an exorcism, I start with the notion: "The demons will do the most despicable, demeaning and awful thing that they can if God allows it."

In previous exorcisms, they have emotionally raped many possessed women at night and even during an exorcism; they have twisted a poor woman's previously wounded leg until she cried out in agony; they threatened a possessed mother's children and taunted them. One time during an exorcism I demanded they answer the question: "If you could, would you stick a knife in the back of everyone in this room, twist it and laugh?" The demons responded with an arrogant, gleeful sneer, "Yes!"

When an exorcism session is finished, it is not uncommon to walk out feeling a bit "slimed," with a bit of the demonic ugliness and filth still clinging to us. A second round of cleansing prayers is often needed. In St.

Faustina's vision of hell, the seventh suffering of hell is despair, hatred of God, vile words, curses and blasphemies. Demons bring this hell with them in an exorcism. Thus, in an exorcism, we experience a taste of hell.

In this life, we are fortunate that the demons are chained. In hell, where the chains are off, it must be infinitely worse. In hell, there is no limit to the evil and torture they can and do inflict. An unpublished manuscript from a Catholic mystic included a vision of hell. His experience was similarly awful beyond description, and very much in agreement with so many others:

"There were millions of them [demons]. There were big ones who seemed like leaders. The smaller ones were obviously their followers. The leaders were more prideful and acted more condescending than others to the humans. The medium and small ones were more physical with the humans—they were asserting their dominance. It was horrible. They asserted their dominance by ripping the skin off the people; they were sticking things in people's eyes; they were doing pretty much any awful thing you can imagine. And they were doing a lot of sexual raping of people and sexually dismembering them. It was just awful. Looking around made me want to vomit. Just watching what the demons were doing made me want to retch. It was so hot that I could hardly breathe, with every attempted breath I felt I was breathing in "stuff" that was causing my insides tremendous pain. I felt as if my flesh would melt right off my arms. Fire engulfed all of the bodies of the souls, the smell of rotting flesh and melting skin was atrocious, so much it made me want to throw up. Where eyes used to be

*in the now damned souls, there was nothing but fire. I
instinctively moved forward to try and help them but
my guardian angel held me back saying: "There is no
help for they who have willfully chosen fire."*

But, an exorcism is not only an experience of hell.
There is also a taste of heaven. We invoke the saints in
heaven and the demons howl. The name of Jesus and
His crucifix are a powerful grace that cowers the evil
ones. Recently, in the midst of a particularly difficult exorcism, I asked the Virgin Mary to come to our aid and
a wide-eyed look of terror came over the demons. In every session there are great moments of grace and a taste
of the Kingdom of Heaven.

Many expect an exorcist and the team to be dour and
perhaps even downcast. After all, going to face-to-face
with the demonic is an ugly experience. This is true.
However, it is likely surprising to many when they encounter our team. To be among us is to feel a bit of the
joy of the Lord. This joy, which is a little taste of heaven,
is very odious to the demons.

A young woman was severely possessed by many
demons. I noticed that whenever she managed to do
something she enjoyed, or at least felt some happiness, the demons would immediately attack her. They
seemed intent on making her miserable. There are many
reasons. In a possessed person there is a melding of consciousness of the demons and the person. The demons
themselves do not want to feel the person's happiness.
In the beginning, all the angels were given full knowledge of what would happen if they rejected God, and
still the fallen angels rejected Him. They chose suffering
and darkness, rather than Divine joy and light. Feeling

the individual's happiness would indeed be odious to the demons and remind them of what they lost.

Also, one of the demons' main goals in the case of a possession is to lead the person into hopelessness and despair. They try to drag the person into their own hellish existence and eventually into hell itself. Truly enjoying God's creation in a healthy and holy way, and rejoicing in the graced company of one's friends would frustrate the demons' plans to infuse misery, isolation, and pain.

I gave another one of our demonically afflicted folks the following daily assignment: "I want you to do something fun every day. It doesn't have to be a big thing, just something you enjoy. Enjoy a walk outdoors; call a friend; read a good book; eat something you like (in moderation), or whatever." Of all the assignments I give her to do in between sessions, this is the one she fails at the most. It is very difficult for her, and important.

Suffering is not good *ipso facto*. Suffering is only good when it is in accord with God's will and thus contributes to one's growth and holiness. Suffering 24/7 is not. A sign of true sanctity is an abiding sense of joy. As St. Teresa of Avila said, "From sour-faced saints, good Lord, deliver us!" One sign that possessed people are getting close to liberation is an increasing sense of joy in their lives. Clearly, the Lord's joy is starting to take hold and the demons' misery is starting to recede.

One of the most satisfying graces for us in this ministry is when the exorcism session is over. The afflicted person, who walked into the center looking ashen, feeling tormented and hopeless, often leaves with a smile, an expression of gratitude, and a feeling of hope, sometimes even joy. It is striking to see the transformation and gives the person and us all a great feeling of hope for this person's future. When the demons are finally definitely cast out, the person will know that joy in an ongoing way.

Compacted into an exorcism is the mystery of redemption: from sin and hell to grace and heaven. It confirms our faith in a very direct, convincing and powerful way. I am blessed to experience the mystery of salvation and our team members have often told me the same. For this grace, and for all of our blessings, we give thanks to God!

Stay in the Boat

Recently I have been sent some "private revelations" from people who claim that Jesus told them that demons can be converted. Some of them are actually engaged in interacting with and praying for demons, thus believing they are facilitating the demons' conversion and entry into heaven. They claim to have often experienced demons converting and entering heaven. As one person told me: "If God is all-powerful and all-merciful, why wouldn't He offer the grace of conversion to the demons and even to Satan?"

But the Church's teaching and long tradition is very clear: "*It is the irrevocable character of their choice, and not a defect in the infinite divine mercy, that makes the angels' sin unforgivable. 'There is no repentance for the angels after their fall, just as there is no repentance for men after death'*" (Catholic Catechism #393).

From the beginning, as noted previously, angels were given an infused knowledge of all the ramifications of rejecting God, yet some chose to do so. It does not make rational sense, but the choice for evil is always against reason.

I often quote an exchange I had with the demons in an exorcism, causing them to face the Truth and thus facilitate their expulsion:

I said, "In Jesus' name, I command you to tell me the truth. Did you make a bad decision in rejecting God?"

With a nasty snarl, the demons responded, "Yes."

I then said, "In Jesus' name, tell me the truth. Are you suffering now because of it?"

Again, a nasty snarl, "Yes."

I said finally, "In Jesus' name, tell the truth. Would you change your decision if you could?"

With an evil emphatic growl the demons said, "No!"

Private revelations of supposed seers must always be subject to the tradition and teaching authority of the Church that Jesus founded and to which he gave his authority. History is replete with misguided visionaries and false prophets. Those who follow these misguided individuals also put themselves in grave spiritual danger.

This recent spate of "private revelations" about converting demons is coming from several different sources and suggests to me that the Evil One is using this as yet another demonic tactic. It is sowing seeds of confusion and doubt, if not downright deception and promoting dangerous spiritual practices. In this case, these individuals, in what must be called their spiritual pride, have ignored the centuries-old teaching of the Church and started to develop a relationship with the demons. The demons are conning them and drawing them deeper into their web and the dark world. I fear for their salvation. Several priests have warned them but they have refused the warning with the response: "I have this straight from Jesus."

The Evil One wants us to engage him and his demons. They are master manipulators. Pope Francis has rightly warned the faithful time and again not to communicate directly with demons. It is even forbidden for

exorcists to converse with demons except in limited circumstances directly related to casting them out. Those
who believe they are listening to Jesus and "converting demons" are likely listening to their own spiritual
fancies at best or, worse yet, to the whispers of Satan.
They are likely in grave spiritual danger and we pray
for them.

This raises a larger and critically important issue.
When engaging in the spiritual combat, and indeed for
all of life, we need to be guided by a sure and reliable
source. I have formally studied theology for several
years before ordination and have continued ongoing
studies for forty years more. I rely on the teachings of Jesus in the Bible, the Ecumenical Councils and teachings
of the Fathers and great theologians. I learn from the
saints and holy mystics, and I rely on the teachings and
guidance of the Popes and my bishop. If ever I believe
something which contradicts these authoritative teachings passed down through two millennia, then the error
must be mine. Who am I to contradict Church teachings
and its saints?

I recently heard one demonologist say, "All demons
are Catholic." I knew what he meant. In the course of an
exorcism, the demons consistently, although inadvertently and indirectly, affirm what the Church teaches.
For example, when we invoke the saints and the demons
howl, they are affirming the Church's teaching about
the communion of saints and their important intercession. When the demons howl in response to Church sacramentals such as holy water, crucifixes, relics of saints,
and other sacramentals, they are affirming the Church's
authority and power to implement these sources of
grace. Demons recognize the power of the priesthood

and the authority of the Church. They cower at the very mention of the Blessed Virgin Mary and they positively hate confession, Mass and communion. Everything the demons do, contrary to their desires, witnesses to the truths taught by the Catholic Church. Yes, all demons are Catholic!

I would add: the demons hate obedience to God, Jesus and his church. Recently in an exorcism, I asked the Blessed Virgin to give the possessed person a double grace of obedience, from her who is supremely obedient. The demons howled.

Obedience is critical in an exorcism. At some point during a long, difficult exorcism, the possessed person almost always comes up against a kind of spiritual wall. They might believe they are receiving a special revelation from God when it is really demonic; or they might be asked to perform a special penance or religious act that they find odious; and/or they might be asked to cut off relationships or stop some practices which are spiritually harmful. They often balk and do not understand why.

For example, one man refused to be obedient to our important admonition of cutting off a harmful relationship. He relapsed and is now demonically worse off than previously. It is critical that the possessed be obedient to the Exorcist. If they do act obediently, they will likely be liberated fairly soon. If they do not, some will relapse and others will simply slip away and don't come back.

All of us need to be obedient. If I, as a priest and an exorcist, do not stay in the Barque (boat) of Peter but launch off doing what is not part of our time-honored tradition and discipline, it will surely end in disaster for me and those to whom I am ministering. Don't start your own church: Jesus already did that. Join his and follow it.

If you stay in the Barque of Peter you will be safe and secure in the teachings of the Bible and the Church. Most assuredly, this boat will weather all demonic storms and bring you safely home.

The Heart of an Exorcist

THE REAL CONFRONTATION BETWEEN AN EXORCIST AND THE DEMONS, ESPECIALLY IN THE MORE DIFFICULT CASES, DOES NOT TAKE PLACE IN THE PRAYER SESSION ITSELF. Satan knows, in a face-to-face fight with Christ and his Church, he loses every time. Rather, his best "game" is behind the scenes.

As a master psychologist, the Evil One tries to manipulate everyone involved—priests, laity, the possessed and family. He tries to make the family break down in discord. He tempts the possessed person to give up. And he very subtly tries to manipulate the priest and team in a myriad of ways.

One of the ways Satan attempts to manipulate the priest is to try to make the priest into his own demonic image: boasting, angry, resentful, punishing, and arrogant. This is a subtle trap for the Exorcist who may feel a tug toward these kinds of demonic emotions, especially when confronting angry, vengeful demons day after day after day.

I received another text from demons last night. Typical demonic rant. The demons were tormenting an afflicted person and her father with a flood of ugly and mocking texts. At one point I texted back the well-known St. Michael prayer. Then, the demonic texts stopped, for a moment. They started up again and a second time I

texted the St. Michael prayer and added, "May the Powers of Heaven surround them, protect them, and cast
out the demons." This time, the demonic bravado and
filth stopped.

The demons signed off with a threat: "It's been a
pleasure Stephen. Maybe tonight, you'll feel my presence surround you as you sleep in what you think is
a serenity (sic), safe-guarded home." Apparently, the
St. Michael prayer was effective against this pack of
demons and I made a mental note to use it again. The
demons did, in fact, "visit" me during the night, but a
quick deliverance prayer cast them out.

In another case, a family was likewise being tormented by hundreds of texts, but this time they are
coming from a witch. She is enraged at them and is
trying to destroy their family. I noticed that there is the
same tone in her texts as found in demonic texts. They
are arrogant, taunting, threatening, lying, and vengeful.
She curses them daily with spells to cause physical and
mental suffering, including their children.

The farther down the dark path someone goes, the
more they think and act like demons. As noted earlier,
we call this: "demon brain." Perhaps this woman began
as a "good" witch, or at least she thought so [there is no
good magic and no good witchcraft]. Now, she is clearly
into black magic and fully under the control of Satan, although she claims she is worshipping a pagan deity. But
she is thinking and acting like demons. She has a case of
complete "demon brain."

All of this reminds me that I must not be like them.
I must always be a follower of Jesus. I must love my
enemies, forgive those who persecute us. I must be
humble and bless all, never curse. The verses below

are an attempt to capture this challenge. These verses are framed and placed prominently in our little exorcism chapel as a reminder to all, but especially for us exorcists:

The Heart of an Exorcist

I do not boast of casting out demons,
boasting comes from the mouths of demons;
I choose to serve the Lord in humility.

I do not feel sorry for my little sufferings,
it is Satan who plays the victim;
I choose gratitude for everything that comes to me.

I do not punish demons or chastise anyone
    for evil deeds,
it is demons who accuse and cause suffering;
I choose to forgive and to heal.

I do not judge the hearts of others,
demons constantly criticize and tear down;
I choose to strengthen and build up.

I do not speak ill of others or curse them,
detraction and cursing is the work of witches
    and demons,
I return a blessing.

I do not hate … even Satan and his minions,
hatred has its home in hell;
I choose to love, my home is in heaven.

Three Case Studies [20]

Her "gods" were Demons[21]

BACKGROUND

THIS WOMAN WAS RAISED CATHOLIC. *Her father told her that Buddha and God are basically the same. She eventually left the faith and enthusiastically practiced Tibetan Buddhism for 35 years. She made vows as a Buddhist nun in India and was yoked to a guru. She did two three-year retreats and even did promotional videos for the community.*

Her guru sexually exploited her for years. She terminated this physical contact, against the wishes of the guru. A number of other young women were similarly abused. This woman believed she had gotten close to "enlightenment" and had a strong kundalini yoga experience.

The leaders of the community and her guru turned against her when their exploitive behaviors were exposed. They threatened her and cursed her. She began to be tormented spiritually and physically by them and their demons. She experienced many ugly physical and mental torments from these gurus. She realized her error and returned to the Faith. She knew she needed help from their evil power and sought out help from the Church.

She contacted Msgr. Rossetti and received many deliverance and exorcism sessions. Over the course of three years, she sent a number of emails which are condensed and excerpted below. The reader might notice a slow, steady progress in her learning and practicing the faith, and increasing liberation from her tormentors.

In the course of the exorcisms, she endured horrendous, daily, demonic attacks and moments of insight and grace. The emails below are a selected, edited sample of a more extensive correspondence and prayer sessions. She has more work to do but she is well on the way to liberation.

[Throughout this case and subsequent cases, Msgr. Rossetti will put in "notes" to the reader to elucidate further what is happening.]

Excerpt 1

[Note: Here is her initial email contact with Msgr. Rossetti]

I'm writing you with a heavy heart. I recently read and loved your book, "An American Exorcist." I was raised Catholic and was very devout as a child. I left the Church when I was 15. My mother had a botched hysterectomy when I was a child and almost died. She received extreme unction, but she survived.

Over the years after receiving the last rites, my mother talked a lot to me about her disillusionment with the Church that did not allow women to use birth control. She had 10 children in quick succession. My mother had a total nervous breakdown, and it took her a few years to recover.

I ended up leaving the Church at age 15 and was agnostic until I encountered Tibetan Buddhism. I officially became a Buddhist. I loved the practice of Chenrezig, the deity of compassion. It reminded me of my early experience of Christ, my first guru. I became more and more enamored of Tibetan Buddhism. I felt there were many parallels with Catholicism.

[Note: She speaks of Christ as if her Tibetan gurus were on a par with him. She is not yet truly a Christian.]

I wanted to immerse myself in meditation and prayer via the tantric methods. I became a Buddhist nun and trained for the traditional three-year, three-month retreat at a Buddhist retreat center. I took my nun's vows in India. Shortly after I took vows, my teacher, who was many years old than me, began a secret sexual relationship with me. This lasted for almost four years and broke my vows. By the time I entered the three-year retreat, our relationship fell apart. I did not feel right about it and did not want to continue the romantic part. He ended up rejecting me as a student almost from the moment the sexual part ended.

I had a lot of problems in that long retreat, but I stayed with it. After it was over, I left and found a new teacher and a new Buddhist community. I did a second three-year retreat. The goal of these long retreats is enlightenment. Due to the obstacle with my former teacher at the first place, I got very close to enlightenment but could not make it. I had some major obstacles followed by an extreme Kundalini awakening that lasted four years.

[Note: She thought she was "very close to enlightenment." It should be noted that her gurus were also supposedly "enlightened." However, her guru was sexually abusing her and eventually tormented and cursed her. It is clear that this path to "enlightenment" is a demonic deception.]

After it stabilized, I experienced a lot of bliss in my subtle body and reached some very refined states of consciousness in meditation. These blissful experiences of mine lasted for many years. I then began to have a series of extremely negative experiences that lasted for many months.

[Note: The Evil One can mimic positive spiritual experiences. Only with proper discernment and recognizing its fruits can one determine the truth. The fruits of these experiences ultimately proved very negative.]

One afternoon, in a waking vision, I saw two younger Buddhist teachers of mine, who are considered highly accomplished tantric Buddhas, perform a wrathful practice against me. They used an effigy. It turns out that they were retaliating for a disclosure at my former Buddhist center. They were blaming me for the outing of my first teacher in a sexual scandal. Other women were also involved in outing him. Their destructive ritual was intended to destroy me both spiritually and physically. They tortured me for many months.

[Note: She had a "waking vision" and, as we shall see, a continuing ability to see her gurus and their demons. This is the "occult third eye." Since she was yoked to demons, this third eye was naturally opened. Part of the full process of liberation will be to cast out the demons and permanently close the occult third eye.]

I was brutalized in a tantric ritual and afterwards felt possessed. The gurus and demons told me ever since that I will go to hell soon. They caused my stomach to expand with air and severe heat burned my body at night. At times I was pressured to commit suicide and ordered to go to hell. I felt that things had gone terribly wrong with the tantric deity and gurus. They were protecting their own, i.e. the elderly lama who was rightly accused of sexual abuse at my former monastery. They targeted me as a scapegoat.

[Note: The vicious actions of these Buddhist teachers clearly demonstrate their evil hearts. The fact that this woman was possessed as a result of their curses and evil demonstrate that these Buddhist teachers were minions of Satan.]

For the past year, I have been terrified and tortured by these gurus and their "deities." Only now I am finding a bit of relief. A friend of mine, a Catholic, has been reciting rosaries for me every day. I too started praying the Hail Mary, but I feel that I am fully possessed by the deity and guru of my Tibetan Buddhist faith. I did invite them into myself years ago and now they control my mind and body. At night my dreams are controlled by a tantric master. He tells me there is no hope, that I sinned according to their creed by having doubts about the guru, and now must go to the worst hell ever. So, it seems to me that this is not a demonic possession, but a very subtle possession by a Buddha. I am powerless against him.

[Note: She does not yet realize that the power the gurus wield is actually coming from demons. She is not possessed by the gurus but rather the demons that they are invoking. Also, we read here the typical signs of "demon brain" and typical demonic messages: "There is no hope for you." "You will go to hell." And eventually they will try to get her to kill herself.

Also, of note, Catholic prayers bring her relief and strengthen her spirit.]

Excerpt 2

They are performing a kind of black magic against me. I know something about this. They don't teach it in the three-year retreat, but it is in the lexicon of the most powerful Lamas. If the accomplished guru believes you have insulted him somehow, or had wrong views about him, he can destroy a person's body, mind, and soul using these shamanic practices.

"In Tibetan practice, effigies are sculpted in the likeness of an enemy or figures drawn on paper into which the practitioner directs the power of a deity or demon that he controls. Such effigies are employed broadly in Tibetan mimetic rituals targeted against enemies, either demonic or human.

There are six operations basic to these rituals: (1) drawing an image or molding a figure resembling the intended target; (2) summoning the target; (3) causing the target's spirit to be absorbed into the image or object; (4) separating the target from its divine protectors; (5) cutting off its life-force to achieve the intended goal; and finally (6) 'liberating' the spirit of the target." The word "liberating" is code for "killing the spirit of the target."[22]

Excerpt 3

[Note: Msgr. Rossetti had told her that her deities were actually demons. She had a hard time believing her gods were demons, despite their black magic and evil curses. Moreover,

she is deeply immersed in Buddhism and still believes what she was taught by them, including their power to send her to hell. She is terrified of it and does not yet fully believe that Christ can protect her from their evil power.]

None of the deities I practiced in my 30 years seemed demonic. They granted powers...to those who did their very exacting practices...I expected to become enlightened in this life...I never thought I would be sent to vajra hell, which is the very worst hell that exists. And like the Catholic hell, it will be for eternity.

Excerpt 4

Is Jesus stronger than anyone, even a tantric Buddha? The one who is attacking me is an emanation of Sakyamuni Buddha. He is possessing me along with his meditational deity. He is human but he can emanate thousands of Buddhas. He can choose the exact place and date of his next rebirth....

The Root Guru is the primary spiritual teacher of a practitioner with whom the practitioner has the deepest spiritual connection and from whom they receive the most important teachings, initiations, and guidance on their path to enlightenment. The Root Guru is often seen as the embodiment of all the Buddhas, bodhisattvas, and lineage masters. The relationship between a student and their Root Guru is central to Vajrayana practice, emphasizing devotion, trust, and respect.

The Root Guru not only imparts knowledge but also provides the necessary blessings and empowerments to progress on the spiritual path. My Root Guru, along with his familiar spirit, a red deity, are attacking me now. I'm sure it is them. Does this mean they are both really demons? I never thought they were before. But then I wonder, why am I suffering so?

I believe I am very subtly possessed by the mind of my Root Guru due to problems I had with a previous teacher and his tutelary deity (or familiar spirit). We all share the same familiar spirit. I was in a three-year-retreat when I ended a romantic relationship with that teacher who was old enough to be my father and who I indeed felt was like a spiritual father to me. That angered him and the retreat became extremely difficult after that.

Now my current teacher and his tutelary deity say they have captured my mind and soul and will drag me to hell for eternity. This is ultimately the opposite of enlightenment. Instead of the mind being opened by the Guru and the deity, they close it down through various mental tortured states.

[Note: She still believes the Buddhist teachings regarding the power of her Root Guru and his evil spirit. She also believes in the goal of "enlightenment" which is not the goal of the Christian. And she is not convinced Christ can free her from their evil power.]

Excerpt 5

I have been doing the prayers for laity on the Catholic Exorcism app and while I feel better, I still have the physical symptoms of possession and at times great fear. It is as if he is completely possessing me.

I hear them at night talking to me from the crown of my head, threatening me about my future and sending me disturbing and disjointed images, sometimes in the form of written messages. They say they will enjoy punishing me. It is such a subtle possession in that he has been possessing me for about 20 years or so in a positive way, waiting to enlighten me. I would often have visions of him, but I didn't realize he was in my mind all the time. Now he wants to silence me because he feels I had a wrong view of him and Buddhism.

Actually, the root cause of this are obstacles in my meditation practice that I experienced in my first three-year retreat with the previous teacher who abused me. Mistakes I made then seem to have derailed any possibility of enlightenment and they have been waiting all these years to turn my current guru against me.

Mind you the one doing this to me is supposed to be a male Buddha (embodiment of loving kindness and compassion) and a female tantric wisdom Buddhist deity who is the main deity in our lineage of practice. I never imagined this kind of cruelty existed in Buddhism.

[Note: She erroneously believed she was having demonic afflictions because of her own mistakes and still believed she was on the proper path to "enlightenment" not realizing that she was only becoming more deeply immersed in their evil. She said she was "subtly possessed" by the gurus and their spirits by giving herself to them years ago as part of her training. Now they have turned against her. It is true that she was possessed by demons because she gave herself over to ones who were truly immersed in evil. But she is starting to realize that something was wrong with the entire experience in recognizing their true cruelty. Her occult third eye is clearly open as she daily perceives her gurus' threats and torments, and their demons.]

Excerpt 6

[Note: She went to confession and Mass in a Catholic Church]

I cried when the priest said prayers absolving me from my sins. I could feel the blessing. After the confession, while waiting for the Mass to begin, I did a bunch of Hail Marys.

I have partaken in Buddhist rituals for so long that it did feel weird to be back in a Catholic Church. I think my possession is very deep. For years it was positive, and I mainly felt it when I participated in Buddhist rituals—I would go into deep and blissful meditations that usually involved all of my chakras with the blissful energy moving up and down my body, and feelings of deep sacredness.

But since the ritual w/effigy, they removed all of that from my body. And they continue to try to scare me at night. As I was dozing off, I saw a big knife and my Root Guru told me that now I should get ready because I needed to die on the New Moon and go to hell. Then I dreamed I saw a funeral procession and people carrying a coffin. He indicated it was my funeral. He said, "Now get ready."

So today is the New Moon. I'm still here. Over the past year, a few times he told me to kill myself on the New Moon. I said I never would do that. Often, I have not known if I would still be alive in the morning or not. I expected he might kill me in the night. He said they were going to. So far it hasn't happened.

You can see how deeply entrenched I have been in this religion. It is actually a very beautiful spiritual path.

This is why I can't understand how this happened to me. I can't understand why my teachers turned against me.

In full disclosure, it will be very hard for me to burn all my Buddhist things now. I would like to wait and see how things go today with the prayers. This all is so recent. I am still grappling with the fact that my Root Guru turned against me.

I want to add that I never lost faith in Jesus Christ. He was a man, Son of God, but he did take birth as a man at one time. And my Root Guru is also a man, but he is a living Buddha. I said a lot of prayers last night before I went to bed. As you suggested I have been doing the *Auxilium Christianorum* prayers every day. I say a lot of other prayers from your app and some prayers and psalms I downloaded from the internet.

[Note: She still equates Jesus and Buddha. She tends to believe in their threats including that they are going to kill her. Msgr. Rossetti often tells her that they do not have the power to kill her. Demons cannot directly kill someone. Thus, they try to make her kill herself. She is still attached to her Buddhist ways and does not want to get rid of all her "Buddhist things." She also still believes the Buddhist way that these gurus were leading her on was a good and holy thing, and if it wasn't for the fact that her gurus turned against her, she would have been "enlightened." What she still cannot believe is that the path to this "enlightenment," which her gurus had already achieved, can only be a path to evil. This is confirmed by their evil actions.]

Excerpt 7

I fell asleep saying the Hail Mary. I had horrible, horrible dreams, and was attacked in my dreams all night: I was shown a knife, was in floods, mocked in my dreams by attackers reciting the Hail Mary etc. I still feel he is controlling my body. He showed me a spider, again, an animal, and said I will never be anything more than that.

I told you I have been threatened with these four things which you said are common in demonic attacks:

1. Told I am worthless
2. Told to kill myself
3. Told I'm going to be tortured in hell for eternity
4. Told there is no hope

Do you think I am possessed? I feel he has control over my body. Last night I was in a deep sleep with the horrible dreams he was giving me and when I began to wake up, I felt he was shooting poison into my head. They said they will give me cancer or a heart attack. I think they are trying to give me brain cancer. He said that he is closing down my mind and that he completely owns my body and mind.

Any advice? I continued to pray this morning to break any bonds and attachments, etc.

The guru who is doing this to me is angry that the exorcism prayers refer to him as a demon.

Excerpt 8

[Note: Msgr. Rossetti asked her to continue with the deliverance prayers and get back to him in two weeks. She still believes they can kill her. She does indeed show strong signs of

being possessed: when the demons possess someone, they have
control over their bodies. Moreover, they can influence their
minds and give them horrible dreams and visions. She does
exhibit these symptoms.]

Okay, I hope they won't kill me before that.

Excerpt 9

It has been about two weeks since the exorcism. I am
still completely possessed by the former Guru and the
Meditational Deity. I feel that the Guru has completely
possessed my body and mind. He can move me at night;
he breathes out of my mouth. Sometimes I hear him/her
breathing on the bed next to me. Last night it sounded
like a hissing snake in the bed—definitely the sound did
not come from me but near me.

Some years ago, I heard a hissing snake above my
head in my room. Actually, it was coming from the area
above my head on the floor behind the bed. There was
no snake in the room, but it was unmistakable. I had
definitely raised the Kundalini energy through the practices in my two long retreats.

Now they are still trying to take me to hell. Interesting that you said demons are not allowed to kill me.
They said they will give me cancer. Are they allowed to
do that?

Excerpt 10

Is God/Jesus more powerful once something has
complete possession of me? They are treating me like
I'm nothing. At night he shows me I will be a spider in
future lives. He laughs at me and mocks me.

My crimes were minute compared to the punishments they have heaped on me. I never would have thought my Guru and meditational deity are using demons, but your statement that they aren't allowed to kill me seems to prove that point.

If not, I'm sure they would have killed me by now.

[Note: As she began to experience that the threats from her Guru and his demons were lies, she started to realize slowly that perhaps Jesus can rescue her from the clutches of this evil, and that she is not doomed to hell because of them.]

Excerpt 11

May we schedule another time for you to pray over me? I have been doing the *Auxilium Christianorum* prayers almost every day and have been saying the prayers on your app most days too. Things are getting worse and worse. The Guru is holding my body and mind. Night is when I feel him the most but during the day he sighs in me. At night he moves my body. He takes over my mind as soon as I fall asleep. He gives me dreams and images. He will put me into a deep sleep state. He relentlessly shows me I will go to hell or be reborn as a bug like a spider or fly. He completely controls me. There is also a deity who is always with him like a protector. She is supposed to be a Buddha, but she wants to take me to hell to torture me. They laugh at the fact that I think the Catholic prayers will help.

Excerpt 12

Thank you very much for scheduling a session this week. I'm coming to my wits end with all this torture.

I have spent 30 years practicing Tibetan Buddhism and cannot believe it has come to this. Buddhism is supposed to be such a peaceful religion, and my Root Guru is supposed to be the embodiment of compassion. He has an extremely powerful mind and says he tried to enlighten me for 20 years but now has had to let me go. He calls me his hostage and says he will cause the total destruction of my mind. I agree with you that this is demonic activity. It is devastating to face this. They themselves don't seem to be concerned about going to hell though. They say that's impossible since they are already enlightened.

[Note: Msgr. Rossetti told her that it is they who are in danger of going to hell and they are aware of his conversations with her through occult knowledge. Her gurus are angry that I called them demons. They equate "salvation" from hell with enlightenment. This is not Christian and obviously a lie.]

Excerpt 13

I said the rosary before I went to sleep. I fell asleep holding the rosary and saying the Hail Mary. After I was asleep for a while, I heard noises coming out of my throat and then I was attacked and strangled. I woke up startled and afraid. Then I heard a woman's voice laughing from the middle of the room. They, my former meditational deity (demon) and guru, think it is hilarious that I think I can be saved by doing the rosary.

I fell back asleep, and she came into my dream and looked at me disgustedly. She and the Guru have been trying to get me to kill myself for over a year, but I would not. Recently she told me to "submit" and "surrender." When I saw her face, she was clearly disgusted that I am still alive and resisting. I told her I did not understand why she is so angry with me as I had done her practice twice in my two retreats (I spent a total of 15 months doing the mantras, visualizations, and complex rituals associated with her practice). I continued to do her practice for years after my retreats. I had not seen her close up like this for a while. She believes I made a grave mistake and broke my commitments and wants me to die so they can reincarnate me in her hell and so she can torture me for eternity.

Excerpt 14

I guess what I'm trying to say is that I was very, very deeply into the occult, but since it was all under the auspices of Buddhism, a supposedly compassionate and peaceful religion, I had no idea what I was getting into.

I'm afraid now because the Guru who is possessing me and the deity/demon were threatening me with death all last year. But death is the least of it. They plan to drag me to hell and torment me forever.

Last night the deliverance prayers felt very powerful. The clenching in my stomach/ribcage got really tight. It feels like being squeezed by a python. During the night I was awoken by a loud sound at the foot of my bed. Then I felt sensations running through my body. It feels like skin crawling. They forced images that I was entrapped in mesh screens. From time-to-time I hear them calling me a demon. It's hard not to be afraid since they don't seem to go away.

[Note: this woman participated in an online deliverance session with Msgr. Rossetti and she felt the power of the Church's deliverance prayers. There are clear moments of grace during this spiritual battle in which Our Lord is guiding her and protecting her. Her physical manifestations and tortures are typical of what demons can do to someone who is possessed. But they are limited in what they can do, despite their threats. They cannot kill someone nor can they give them cancer or a heart attack, despite what they threaten. But they can choke someone and often do so in exorcism sessions.]

Excerpt 15

My parish priest, who is a very fine and well-educated priest, told me he doesn't believe in possession really. He thinks it is almost always a mental illness. He has a BA in psychology and an MA in philosophy and theology.

The problem is that the attacks at night are getting really bad again. They are causing my body to become paralyzed so I can't get up. It's very hard to shake it off. They bombard me with horrible threats and images all night long, completely control my dreams, cause my stomach to fill up with air on and off, and then expel it violently. They laugh and mock me and move my fingers, arm, and legs and cause my toes to twitch. I know now that fallen angels reinvented themselves as tantric deities. So many have fallen that way.

I can receive communion but after the Stations of the Cross two weeks ago I became violently ill. It feels like possession to me because so much of my body is under their influence. I just awoke because I was making a groaning sound in my sleep. I felt something splash on the top of my head, like water and then felt it dripping.

I told you before that they have an effigy of me with which they tortured me for the first year and now they are still using it. Weird stuff is happening. They are still doing black magic against me. I am afraid.

[Note: Her fear empowers the demons. Msgr. Rossetti keeps assuring her that Jesus is Lord and that she needs to trust him. Sadly, her parish priest is no help and actually his disbelief can be harmful to someone in this woman's situation.]

Excerpt 16

The female sensitive who attended our next to last exorcism session said that she felt I was giving them [the guru and demons] too much power. What no one seems to understand is that I gave them my power 35 years ago and they still have it. And even if I try to take back my power, they are still wielding power over me. And also, I know that they can send illness and disease. It happened to three other women I knew very well. They all three got cancer from a lama and this deity/demon. One of them has already died. I helped to take care of her for a brief time before she had to go into intensive care. Her husband told me that our common former guru had been harassing both of them for years, including either causing her cancer or the conditions for it. I have turned to Christ and the Virgin. But these others wield a lot of power because I bound myself to them not knowing who they really were.

So, they have told me they will give me a heart attack and cancer. I have been taking an online RCIA course. I have been taking a course, "Explaining the Faith," on YouTube. It is a wonderful and a very extensive course.

I am still working on the RCIA course, but I know I need to step it up.

[Note: Msgr. Rossetti's experience as an exorcist is that demons cannot give someone cancer or heart attacks although they can stress someone to the point where the person might naturally develop a physical ailment. Thus, trusting in Jesus is critical! Moreover, this woman also does not understand that although she gave herself to the evil gurus and their demons, when she turns to Jesus, Jesus can and does break the evil connection. Thus, we often prayed to break these evil "soul ties" as part of the exorcism. But it is a process; it is not one and done, especially with someone who spent decades in the grip of demons.]

Excerpt 17

I am writing with a heavy heart. Having in-person exorcisms, the demon manifested, and I am either possessed or severely oppressed. It has definitely helped, but the demons haven't left yet.

The Guru still has control over my subconscious thoughts and dreams and still tortures me. The red female demon is still inside me. I can feel her in the form of energetic sensations, or sometimes she makes her presence known in other ways.

It feels like I am inside the Guru's mind stream, that I am his prisoner and have become a part of his mind. He constantly shows me being zipped up in small compartments where he will keep me. I hear him breathing in me and feel his presence inside of me every night. Even my dreams come from him, and all the thoughts and images I have when I am in the space between waking and sleeping are images injected into my mind by him. It often feels quite seamless. I will think it is my own thought and then realize it came from him.

During the day I am functional but don't have control over my body. It feels like there is a very powerful balloon inside my body and he injects air into my anus and my stomach blows up. I can feel the air coming in.

I go to Mass almost every day, say the rosary daily, and pray to Jesus often, asking for his help and deliverance. But the Guru is always there within my mind, or I am within his. He can still move my body at will or makes noises in or around my body.

I don't know why I can't feel the presence of Jesus Christ or why these entities haven't been expelled. I was tricked and deceived into believing that Buddha was the same as God. The Tibetan Buddhist religion is encased in a blanket of sanctity so people can't see that it is actually satanic. Tantra is satanic.

Because this has control over my mind and body, I feel dehumanized and almost completely different from who I always was. I am losing hope. I never had an abortion or killed anyone and have been celibate for many years. Everything that is happening to me is due to the anger and whim of my previous guru who was sexually using his nuns. When I tried to end that sexual relationship because it felt wrong, that guru started cursing me. Even though I left him and found another teacher, eventually that first teacher and his familiar demon won, and they did the rituals to destroy me.

Do you have any advice? I'm losing hope. I attend your sessions every month.

*[Note: One of the great challenges for someone who is pos-
sessed is to trust in Jesus and trust that He will free you in
time. But it is a process. This woman was into these non-Christian practices for over 30 years and she gave herself to these
individuals and their demons. Her spiritual state was similar
to someone who joined a Satanic cult and made an explicit
blood contract with Satan. The process of liberation will be
long and slow.]*

Excerpt 18

The exorcism sessions we just did helped a lot. It put
more of a buffer between me and the demons. They haven't left but my fear abated, and I feel hope again. The
last two nights, my dreams were neutral, and dare I say
that last night my dreams were almost pleasant and that
is rare.

I felt the demon manifest during our exorcism session, which I think is a good thing. She told me later
that night that I had made "a promise" to her. She is
deeply embedded in my subtle body, it's obvious. I feel
like I have a creature living within me. There is always
squeezing in my torso and at the same time, pressure
from within pushing outwards—an energy protruding
in my abdomen as if there is something living there. It
breathes within my chest and moves around my body.
When that happens, it feels like strange energetic prick-
ling and rippling sensations under the skin. I will double down on my prayers and devotions again. I have a
lot of work to do on myself. I need to do regular fasts.

Are pagan gods really demons? It would be good
to know more about how the pagan gods are really demons. In terms of the oppression, I'm still not free but

the omnipresent fear lifted. I feel more connected to Christ and am feeling more genuinely connected to Catholicism than I have since I converted back three years ago. The demon is still very much there, especially felt at night, but it's definitely getting weaker. I am attending your monthly online sessions and that helps a lot. I continue to feel better although I am still oppressed but it's much less frightening.

[Note: She has spiritually turned a corner and is starting to be hopeful and feel connected to Christ and the faith. It has taken three years of holy living and both in person exorcism and online deliverance sessions to get this far. However, she will continue to struggle with hope as the torments continue and their mockery and taunts affect her thinking. But the prayers are starting to have an obvious effect in giving her some relief. This suggests that the demonic hold over her is weakening.]

Excerpt 19

Yesterday's online deliverance seminar and prayer was very powerful. I really benefited from the retreat. Thank you! Something happened last night that may be significant, or not, as we know the demons lie. For quite a while now when I am attacked at night, I do the casting out prayers preceded by stating the authority of my baptism in the Father, Son, and Holy Ghost. I usually follow the casting out prayers by "Our Fathers" and/ or "Hail Marys." It usually works, and after a while the attacks subside, and I am able to sleep peacefully.

Last night, I woke up around 2 am because I heard very loud knocking around my head. It sounded external, like someone was knocking on my window, but much closer. The intent was clearly to wake me up. I was afraid and got up for a little while. After about an hour, I fell asleep again and saw the red demon several times, very close up. I saw her eyes, her lashes, her outfits, etc. She kept coming and going. Then she started singing as she sometimes does. The song had these words, "I'm tired of being hurt," and she said something to the effect that she was going to leave soon.

Excerpt 20

Buddhism has an ethical system somewhat like Christianity (for instance, they believe that abortion is killing). Many people have been fooled by the seemingly peaceful and beneficial Buddhist teachings such as mindfulness and compassion. It is only much later that we realize there are demonic underpinnings to it all.

I'm lying here with the demon inside of me. I can feel her moving around all the time. It feels like a sickening, toxic wind. It feels like metal clamps are around my ribcage and chest squeezing me to death. I can sometimes hear them faintly from the very top of my hair mocking me.

If I close my eyes for a minute, the Guru shows me I am encased in nets that he constantly tightens and then he will start putting disturbing images into my mind. His favorite thing is to dehumanize me and show me that I am his prisoner and can never escape. He breathes in me on and off throughout the day. I especially feel it at night or when I am resting. It feels like another person is breathing in me. Or that I am contained within him, as if he has swallowed me and is possessing me at the same time. Or maybe he is astral projecting into my body. He is even more of a presence than the demon, because she does seem to retreat when I pray. I am not crazy. This is really happening.

It really hurts and I don't know what else to do. I have repented again and again and called out to God for help. All I hear is them laughing or sighing in frustration. I guess this is because of all the guru yoga practice I did in retreat and the extreme physical and breath yoga that created a home for the demons inside of me. It is quite lonely being tortured by the demon and my former guru. It's unimaginable. Sorry to complain, but I am starting to lose hope again. I wonder why it is so hard. He tells me I will never be free because I am already part of his mind stream.

I was up most of the night saying casting out prayers and then fell asleep and the Root Guru tried to suffocate me. I woke up with a terrible headache and realized that they are trying to kill me.

It helps to do the prayers, but they just retreat or go quiet for a little while. But the Guru is always there. I am bound to him. Last night I began to think there is no way to get free of him and for the first time I almost thought of giving up.

Of course, I am in a completely different place than I was when I first reached out to you three years ago, thanks again for that.

Excerpt 21

When I received your text yesterday, I was at an extremely low point. I hadn't been able to sleep the night before, so I was trying to rest and take a nap, but I was being attacked internally. They use an effigy or voodoo doll, and I felt like they were injecting acid into my stomach, chest, and esophagus. The night before the Guru tried to strangle and suffocate me and I started to think there was no hope. When this started, he told me I had to kill myself as they would never give up and I was as good as dead.

When I refused to kill myself, he was very angry and accused me of inconveniencing them by hanging on until the "bitter end." It's so strange that demons feel they own us and have the right to command us to die.

After our prayer session yesterday, I immediately felt better psychologically. I experienced some physical retaliation such as extreme heat in my torso and movements of the demon, but the acid attacks stopped. After the sessions throughout the day, as the afternoon and evening progressed, I felt better and better. Psychologically I felt lighter and more hopeful. Physically I felt more at ease. Last night I fell asleep peacefully and had neutral dreams and slept very well until now.

The Guru says I am within him and joined with his mind so there is no way to be free. The demon is very deeply integrated with my energy body. It's hard not to despair. I pray to God and Jesus all night, but I just hear his [the Guru's] voice and feel his presence within and without me.

Thank you so much for praying over/with me. Of course, it helped in the short run as always by having a peaceful night and renewed feelings of hope. I think it made an impact on the demons that was significant. The night of the Deliverance prayers, the Guru appeared in a dream, and I implored him to stop torturing me and others and to start practicing true compassion and peace like Christ. Next morning when I said the Rosary, I kept yawning hugely and couldn't stop. Not from boredom or sleepiness but because it was having some effect on the demon/s. I felt like I had more control over my mind again, although that could just be a temporary ruse on their parts. But overall, your prayers seemed to have a significant impact.

Thanks again. I'm trying to go to Mass 5 or 6 days a week and listening to lectures about St. Thomas Aquinas and others and generally trying to get more deeply into the life and thought of the Catholic Church.

Except 22

Yes, I know Jesus is Lord and I should not cede any power to them. But in their system, they have destroyed me.... I didn't get enlightened when I was supposed to. Then many Tibetan lamas, including my root guru, were exposed for sexual abuse and they became extremely angry and wanted revenge against the women exposing them. The Tibetans are very clannish and take these things very personally because that lama we exposed was a "made man." It works like the mafia.

The reason why I must be destroyed and killed is a legal demonic one. The demon and that sorcerer did not forget the mistakes I made in their system, and she is the one in charge of all of them. My Guru tried to "enlighten me" in my second retreat as well as one of the tantric masters who is now doing this ritual against me, but the demon didn't allow it to happen.

When you don't become enlightened either because the demon doesn't like you or because you made a mistake in your practice or in your *samaya* [sacred bond] with the lama, the result is ritual murder. Thus, one must be taken out, driven insane, forced to kill oneself or else they try to kill you. This is because of the tantric law—they say that practicing tantra is like being a snake in a bamboo tube, you either go up (to enlightenment) or down to vajra hell (this is when they capture the consciousness in their nets and destroy it).

Being as demons are very legalistic, this is something that must happen. My Guru says he kept trying to enlighten me for 20 years after retreat (to avoid this ritual murder), but I didn't accomplish the practice. The demon told me that she didn't allow me to accomplish the practice (she is bound to the mind). Thus, I was trapped in a weird Catch 22. I am possessed by her through years of initiations and rituals.

If you have read this far, all I can say is that these are the "deep things of Satan." My Guru stopped protecting me when I started to have doubts about him and the whole tantric path, wondering if it was Luciferian at core. They told me they were taking me out. They said: "You know too much," among many other things.

That is just their arcane set of tantric laws. We aren't sufficiently warned about this possibility because if they told Westerners about this before we did the three-year retreat, no one would ever do it.

The mental attacks are frequent and frightening. And physically I don't feel well most of the time but I'm functional and can work and study so that's good. And I'm grateful for how far I have come.

[Note: She still hangs onto their ideas about enlightenment and the power they claim to have over someone's soul. This is not good. It cedes more power to the demons. It will take a long time to expunge her non-Christian ideas after over 30

years of intensely living their teachings. If their gurus and teachers had achieved "enlightenment" as she claims, then it can and must be a demonic ruse, given their sexual abuse of their female disciples, and relentless torturing of her and these other women.]

Excerpt 23

For the last few nights, I have been under their focused and targeted attack. Yesterday while resting I felt them moving in my chest cavity and throat. They were making noises and manipulating that area. Last night it was the most intense pain that went on and on radiating from my heart to my head. I was countering it with casting out prayers through the authority of my baptism in the Father, Son, and Holy Spirit and through "Our Fathers" and "Hail Marys." It went on for a long time, not stopping, not responding to my prayers. Finally, it quieted down and I fell asleep.

This Guru is a very powerful sorcerer. The Red Demon is a very powerful spirit. They are calculated and deadly. I'm not afraid of them, or afraid of dying, but I know they will not stop this until I am dead. I am afraid that they have captured my soul. I believe in God and in Jesus and have received so many blessings from them but it's hard to be under such intense attack for so long. He [the Root Guru] is strong and will never stop.

Excerpt 24

Just giving you an update on my situation. In Adoration yesterday I prayed the Deliverance prayers for the Laity on your app. They are very profound. Thank you for offering to pray over me today. I am not feeling well at all and have some commitments later so I can't do it today.

[Note: Msgr. Rossetti was counseling her not to give so much power to her torturers; they are feeding off her fear.]

I try not to give them any power, but they forcefully inject degrading images and sometimes written messages. I must constantly combat them and bat them away, and then they move inside of me and make noises and sensations to mock me. They growl and carry on. It's ongoing but occasionally they pile it on to the max, so I'll feel unnerved, exhausted, and defeated.

I believe everything you say about them being mere dust compared to Jesus. It's just they are so insidious. I will continue to pray and have faith.

Excerpt 25

[Note: She had a positive spiritual experience on Divine Mercy Sunday.]

On Divine Mercy Sunday at the Shrine, something unusual happened with my rosary. I had owned the rosary for about a year, but it never seemed special to me. The centerpiece was a plain silver triangle with a crudely embossed carved head. After a priest blessed it, I used it regularly, even though I still found it subpar.

During the Mass, I suddenly felt compelled to take out the rosary and noticed something strange. The centerpiece, which had always seemed vague and unattractive, now clearly depicted Christ with His Sacred

Heart and rays of light. It was lovely, an elegantly carved image with a detailed border.

Puzzled at the sudden transformation, I spoke to the priest who had blessed the rosary a year earlier. After hearing my story, he suggested that a demon might have been blocking my perception, preventing me from seeing the true image on the rosary. He believed that the grace from the Divine Mercy Mass had removed this obstacle.

This experience reminded me of a man's story about how his involvement in Freemasonry had caused him to experience spiritual blindness for many years. Like him, my involvement in the occult clouded my ability to connect with the Catholic faith.

After this incident, praying the rosary became much easier and more meaningful for me. What once felt like a struggle now feels much more natural.

Excerpt 26

Since I got home from the exorcism sessions four days ago, I have been very, very tired. I took a nap that first afternoon and heard deep growling within, (this happens on and off) and then in a sort of dream state I saw a snake emerge from a body of water enough to show its head and part of its neck. Still extremely drowsy, I could not fully wake up. Next, I saw the red demon from the back. Then it turned around with long, dark flowing hair. It had a sinister sneer on its face and was wearing a large crucifix! It was clearly mocking the prayer session earlier in the day. After that dissolved, I saw a text screen with the words, "I will leave on...." but the text disappeared before I could read the rest of that message. That felt mocking too, as it probably really has no intention of leaving. What was significant though was how much the Latin prayer disturbed it and how it responded.

During the major exorcism prayers, we all noticed that the demon reacted strongly to the "Litany of the Saints," in particular to St. Elijah, St. Joseph, Mother Theresa, and the relics of Pope John Paul II. In the Bible, St. Elijah was key in casting out the prophets of Baal. I read somewhere and saw photos showing that Baal and Shiva had similar iconography. I wonder if they are essentially the same demon, but I have no definitive proof.

I am back home and I'm feeling very good. The Guru did assert himself last night. He came up to my throat and growled (internally) twice last night but I just rebuked him in Jesus's name and went to sleep.

I feel very, very blessed after the last two days of exorcisms. I have a lot of confidence now that they are weak demons and that the stuff they are doing is just harassment and not to worry too much about it but just keep trying to become more sanctified. The Red Demon is beaten down for now. I felt the Root Guru demon assert himself today in Mass and even just now as I'm writing this. He is very arrogant. But I'm not going to give into fear. I know that Christ is stronger. In the future, I would love to do a pilgrimage of Marian sites in Europe and go to the Guadalupe site in Mexico. I also would like to go to Italy and visit some holy places and do Catholic pilgrimages. I think that will help a lot.

Following the exorcism, I felt incredibly enriched and blessed by my time with you and your team. The peaceful feelings following those sessions lingered a long time and my faith in Christ and the sacraments deepened. Although I am still not completely free of the demons, I feel more at peace than ever before. I hope and pray that one day I shall be completely free and healed by the grace and mercy of our Lord Jesus Christ.

I am now one-hundred percent certain that demons lurk behind the practices of Eastern mysticism. I regret ever encountering Tibetan Buddhism. I was so wrong, so misled. As you told me in our first meeting, "They aren't buddhas, but demons posing as buddhas." How true that is! I am very grateful to you and to your team. It was an extraordinarily blessed experience. I'm so lucky. I appreciate you all so much.

EPILOGUE

Her last entry well explains her progress. After over three years of prayer and living the Catholic faith, the demonic hold over her is much weakened. The Catholic faith and teachings are more rooted in her. She is less afraid and more trusting in Jesus, which helps to weaken the demons. She is not fully liberated but well on the way. Given her extensive history of involvement with them, full liberation will be a long process. But she is able to work now and is starting to be hopeful and creative. In short, she has gotten her life back. Thanks be to God!

Possessed by the New Age[23]

BACKGROUND

THE FOLLOWING IS A NARRATIVE FROM A WOMAN WHO SUFFERED SEVERE DEMONIC ATTACKS. *She describes her journey from Catholicism into New Age spiritualities. She suffered psychological wounds as a child with her parents' divorce and also being bullied in school. She encountered unidentified spirits as a child and opened herself to these spirits thinking they might be friendly. Her mother introduced her to New Age spiritualities. She was heavily involved in many kinds of divination, alternative spiritualities, and occult activities for a number of years. As she became more deeply involved in the New Age, the darkness and depression in her life increased to the point where it became difficult for her to function. She had a powerful spiritual experience of Jesus which was life-changing. Here is her story....*

[Throughout the narrative, Msgr. Rossetti will make comments to the reader to explain what is happening.]

As a child, I was baptized in a Catholic church. In my early childhood, my mother and I both went to a Catholic church nearby for Sunday Mass. But there were many outside spiritual interests and one day we just stopped going....

When I was four, my parents divorced. There were many conflicts between them. The conflicts gradually got worse as I grew older which put me under a lot of pressure. I experienced a lot of bullying both in kindergarten and in the first years of elementary school. I often played on my own because the other children didn't want to be with me. Thoughts about an "other world" became quite appealing to me.

[Note: Early psychic wounds can create a vulnerability to demonic influences.]

I remember walking alone in a small wood nearby to where I lived when a tree seemed to come alive and I had the strong feeling that I could actually talk to it. I was around 7 or 8 at the time. It was about this time that I felt that something spiritual was trying to contact me. It was pushing softly on me as I was trying to sleep in the evening. I remember not liking it too much. But then I thought it might be one of my deceased ancestors so I opened up to it a bit....

[Note: It does happen that young children can be influenced and even possessed by an evil spirit, particularly if they open themselves to such spirits, as it appears this woman did as a child.]

When I was around 12-years-old my mother became interested in New Age spirituality. Books about Eastern mysticism and astrology had always been around, but there were now many new titles. I had also been quite interested in "super-natural" things and psychic phenomena for quite a while. I think I always had some sort of awareness of the spiritual world. I would often "sense" things and "feel" if the energy in a room was off or if there was something wrong about a person.

At about 15 years of age, I started eating at the local krishna restaurant with my mother. This food is called "prasad" which means "gift" in sanskrit, and has been offered to an idol before serving it to customers. There is a whole religion around food connected with krishna and bhakti yoga. To this day, I still at times sense the smell from that food around me and have spiritual intrusions in my soul and body because of this.

[Note: It is not uncommon that children will come under the influence of evil spirits through the malfeasance of their parents. In this case, her mother introduced her into non-Christian spiritualities and had her regularly eat food offered to idols.]

At University, I was supposed to study, but I got a bad depression. This depression had been lurking in my mind since I was around 12-years-old, with mood swings and self-loathing. But when I was 19, my depressions got worse. I couldn't concentrate when I was trying to study. It felt like something was attacking me with a violent sense of meaninglessness and emptiness. I didn't understand what was happening to me. I had been very good at school. But now I couldn't understand anything. I would read the same sentences over and over, but they wouldn't mean anything to me.

I started to wonder whether I wanted to explore a more "creative" way of life. I believed I had been too much of a kind and obedient girl. I started to rebel against the status quo and against my parents. I thought that everything about society basically was wrong and

I started to defy my parents thinking that everything they represented was false and boring. I was completely lacking in humility and at the same time very lowly and depressed.

I got a job and started earning some money. I spent it all on clothes. I started to put too much focus on looks. I wanted to go out dancing and things like that. I was still very lonely. I always felt lonely, even when there were people around me.

[Note: It is likely she was already being significantly influenced by evil spirits, given the negative influences in her childhood.]

It was at this time that I had a strange experience. I was standing at a crossroads near to where I lived. Suddenly I felt or heard a booming male voice inside me or maybe around me which warned me against the road I was about to take. It literally beckoned me to walk the straight and narrow path and not walk that other road—the one towards a "crazy" lifestyle. It told me that I should continue to be a prudent and rational person and not continue on the path to destruction. I ignored this voice. I basically had two thoughts about it: 1) that I had imagined it or 2) that it was God's voice and that He sounded too demanding and strict.

Some time later, I heard and felt this voice again. I was having one of those bad days, and I felt that God was warning me against focusing so much on clothes and on superficial things. I felt that it was the voice of a concerned Father. But I didn't want to listen. On one hand I didn't take it seriously, and I thought it sounded too "patriarchic."

At this point I had completely closed the door to the Christian faith but one thing that remained was a strong influence of our Mother Mary. I felt a magnetic attraction for her. I would suddenly long so much for her. I felt like I just had to have a medallion on me with her picture on it. I had seen one in a jewelry shop but when I went there it had been sold. I ended up buying a medallion with buddha on it instead because that was all they had left in the shop. Although in my mind I thought "it's just about the same thing" because in New Age "it's all one" anyway, although in my heart I felt sad.

I had many people around me who were into alternative spiritual ways. I remember reading my first book that channeled spiritual beings. I ended up buying into the ideas it represented. It presented New Age ideas, that is, a completely "new" spirituality which was something quite different from Christianity. It talked a lot about what happens after death. According to this philosophy, there is no hell. There is no punishment. There is only the "mind."

The ideas in the book centered a lot around opening one's mind. It contained New Age slogans such as: "It's all love" and "We are all one." According to this philosophy Christians are all caught up in their own moralizing "black and white" way of seeing things. There is no right or wrong; ultimately there is only love. I swallowed these ideas and adopted them. They suited me. But my depressions and the confusion of my life only got worse. I saw a psychic who said many things. She was right about many of them. That started my interest in divination and psychics.

[Note: Her depressions are likely a barometer of her spiritual health. As she moved deeper and deeper into the New Age and spiritual darkness, her depressions got worse.]

During that time, most of my friendships were turbulent and difficult. There was a bohemian undertone to the parties I attended. I was in a long-term romantic relationship and we had a child. But the child's father was abusive and it was a very difficult time for me both during our relationship and when we split up. I went into a deep crisis because the child's father became threatening and almost psychotic in his behavior. I was very scared. I started doing tarot card readings to get answers for myself about this situation and other problems in my life. It seemed to calm me down.

I started with Doreen Virtue's oracle cards. Particularly it was a book of hers about "Angel healing" that got me interested in her, her oracle cards and general philosophy. I read most of her books and I bought many of her oracle card decks. I used them for all kinds of questions that I could have during a day. (An interesting sidenote is that Doreen Virtue has had a big conversion to Christianity and is now an on-fire Christian advocating against all kinds of New Age practices.) After that I continued with all sorts of oracle and tarot card decks.

[Note: These practices of divination are a very clear opening to the demonic. Divination is a very serious sin and the Bible calls it an "abomination." It is a serious and potentially devastating violation of the First Commandment. Its negative spiritual impact should not be underestimated.]

I started practicing shamanism, going on healing courses with a shaman and going on "journeys" to discover my "power animal" while listening to pre-recorded drumming on-tape. During these "travels" I would sometimes have experiences that seemed not of this world, such as seeing my power animal interiorly, and having glimpses of a big inner lake.

When I was 23, I was introduced to a yoga sect. During the first satsang meditation, I had a spiritual experience which made me want to come back. But I didn't like the people there and I had a deep aversion towards the picture of a woman who was a guru that everyone seemed to be worshipping. But I trusted the leader and her story of having her life turned around through this guru.

One woman there was having uncontrollable shaking movements along her spine as she was sitting in a lotus position in front of the image of the guru. She shook violently while we chanted. I thought it was strange and disturbing but never would have guessed that it was demonic. I always knew something was wrong, such as when I had my first "real" meditation experience with this sect. I had an experience where I fell into the wrong sort of "well" inside of me. I also had a vision of a temple inside me. All of these experiences had a darkness and a gloominess about them which I now know was satanic. At that time I just felt unsure about what to do with it and whether to continue on or not. I didn't believe that the devil was real anyway.

This unsureness made me keep on searching for the answer in other places too. I kept calling on clairvoyants. One of them was very talented and could see many things in my room, like she was actually there, although I was talking with her on the phone. She said she thought I had "abilities" myself.

[Note: Many people with such spiritual "abilities" actually have their "occult third eye" opened. They have an ability to see into the demonic world because of the presence of demons in their own lives. Part of the liberation process is to cast out these demons and close the occult third eye.]

After about 7 years, I decided that I would get more serious with yoga. I had a friend who was very much into a form of kundalini yoga and she taught me a bit of it too. Here too there were supernatural experiences with images of gurus in my mind, and with inner lights. After a long time of doing their mantras, meditations every day, and of partaking in satsangs on a weekly basis and going on retreats, I had a very bad demonic experience. I didn't understand what it was. But I had already had many supernatural experiences with them which I now know were demonic, such as the movement of the kundalini serpent at the bottom of my spine. Sometimes the floor would tremble—literally. And inner lights and smells of the incense they used a lot would appear to my inner senses.

But one day after what seemed to me to be a "kundalini rising" experience, I had a horrible beeping sound in my ear that wouldn't leave. I desperately thought: "Is there a way I can reverse this experience?" It seemed hellish. But I still thought that this yoga sect was the only answer and the truth.

These supernatural experiences weren't all negative. In fact, they were mostly very positive. There would be nice smells, feelings and special "graces" such as flights of the soul to "other realms", inner images and lights. I wouldn't have been into these things unless it felt like it paid off somehow. I would also experience healings of physical illness and "miracles" such as money that would appear in my account when I needed it the most.

[Note: Demons can fake positive spiritual experiences. This deceives practitioners into thinking they are doing something good. It leads them deeper and deeper into the dark world and strengthens the bonds between these practitioners and demons.]

"Kundalini rising" is the ultimate goal of all yoga schools, systems and traditions. It is the energy at the bottom of the spine, the kundalini snake, which rises and passes through what is called the "central channel" thereby opening all the chakras on the way before finally reaching the top of the head and leading to "enlightenment."

[Note: Msgr. Rossetti: "I continue to be amazed that people think having a snake wrapped around their spine and traveling up to their heads is a good idea."]

At first, I didn't understand what had happened to me. I only knew that the experience I had was connected to the yoga practices that I had been doing and that I wanted it to stop. Then I realized it probably had something to do with the kundalini. I researched it and realized that many people have gone mad and gone to psychiatric hospital after dabbling with the kundalini and especially these "kundalini rising experiences."

But I kept on being interested in yoga and in all things pagan including witches and wicca. I think the reason why the yoga demons seem to bother me so much even today is because I immersed myself so completely in it—thinking it was the truth. I always kept a bit of skepticism about witchcraft, and I took pride in never being interested in contacting demons—"who would ever want that" I thought to myself. I thought one could be a "good" witch—or a bad one. The good one would only contact good spirits, but I wasn't quite sure who these "good" spirits were. In my head they were a mix of angels, deities and nature spirits.

I now realize that the spirits of the New Age deities cannot be good because they are fallen angels pretending to be something they are not. But whenever I came across these kinds of opinions, I got angry. I thought to myself that these Christians were intolerant and also very paranoid. I thought that Christians were obsessed with the devil and that they were actually bringing in darkness and demons by focusing so much on evil. I know that many practitioners of witchcraft also think that way because they told me.

I ended up moving to a small village which is a center of New Age spirituality. There was a lot of occult activity going on there connected to Europeans myths, druids, goddesses and many other occult practices and witchcraft. Most of the "alternatives" living there actually believe that this mythical realm is a real place and that this village is a place where one can come to be healed because of this supernatural reality. In addition to it being a center of witchcraft, it is connected to a big druid hill in the midst of town and it attracts all kinds of esoteric schools from all the world including many forms of yoga, krishna worship, cathars, druids and others.

So much happened in this place, including my conversion back to Jesus. This town was a very important pilgrim town in the Middle Ages. It is considered to be the actual birthplace of the Catholic church of that country, but this is so long ago that it's all shrouded in myth. It's still a Marian Shrine which it has been for many hundreds of years. So the Christian element was always there. And this seemed right to me as I considered it to be "all one."

I had many extreme experiences in this town when it comes to the supernatural. As I moved to this town, the first thing I did was to knock on a witch's door. I had stayed at her bed and breakfast place many times before. I liked her very much; I admired her. She was charismatic but with a terrible temper. I had had a bad feeling about contacting her and the sinking feeling kept increasing. But now it seemed too late to turn around. I had quit my job and left everything in order to begin a new life in this town. I went there because I was looking for holiness in life. I thought that the new paganism, yoga and the New Age, would give it. I was wrong. When I started realizing this, something very bad started happening in the spiritual realm.

First of all, since my move to this place, the spirits that I had already been in contact with changed from gentle behavior to very intrusive. On my previous six or seven visits to this town, these spirits seemed like angels to me. They made my life seem very sweet and safe. But now, many nights I dreamt that they were actually trying to "break into me." Many other people around me who lived in the same town would tell of similar experiences, which were disconcerting to them. I think we all blamed the practitioners of "bad" witchcraft, but no one really understood why this was happening.

[Note: It is noteworthy that the demons which formerly were "gentle" and made her feel "sweet," now started to be "very intrusive" and she felt they were trying to "break into" her, i.e., possess her. Not uncommonly demons will initially seem positive and loving, and only later, after a bond is created, begin to show their true selves. They then become vicious and possessive.]

The followers of Krishna were very prominent in this town. I had already for many years been eating food from the local Krishna restaurant in my hometown. This food has been offered to demons (Krishna and his consort, Radha). Krishna actually means "the dark one." People have many positive spiritual experiences with Krishna and with other deities that are being called on. But these experiences are nice only for a while. In my case they left me empty and unfulfilled in the long run.

When I moved to this town, I started to see through the charade. Many people that I knew there were finding flats and jobs and having all kinds of opportunities in this place where "the energies" seemed so strong. I too received some "favors" from the "spirit of the place." Clearly there was some kind of spiritual power behind these happenings. But many of these people were behaving quite immorally being unfaithful to their partners, and also generally not being kind to one another. Many were deep into drugs and other vices. Because of this I started to question whether the power behind all these "good things" coming to them wasn't good at all.

[Note: "By their fruits, you shall know them."]

As I started seeing through the spiritual charade of the New Age and in particular of the "goddess," I also started turning more and more towards Christianity. It happened very slowly and not without the help of the only true Lady, our blessed Mother Mary. The goddess worship of this town was associated with a temple with its own priestesses. I went to their temple regularly to rest and meditate. I often had meditation experiences there similar to the ones I had in the yoga sect including complete darkness and feeling like a stone at the bottom of the sea. I wondered how come the two experiences could be so like one another. Now I know it's the same source—the Evil One. But still these experiences had a very pleasurable side to them; I felt almost intoxicated with a sense of calm and of a feeling of relaxation.

This sect of goddess-themed worship had a sort of toxic feminism which was against men in general. Many of the women there had been hurt by men, and perhaps this was part of the attraction. A part of this healing journey was an entering into an "original wildness." Somehow our modern world was seen to hurt this wildness which was seen as a higher good in itself. Connected to this was also a sort of militant eco-warriorship. The wildness of nature and the wildness of "the woman" and "the goddess" (gaia, hecate, the whole Egyptian and Celtic female pantheon, etc.) were seen as one and the same. According to my understanding "they" (being the capitalist forces, "men in suits", the school system, any system in particular, Christians and the church in general) were seen as enemies of this primeval wildness.

After a year–and–a-half in this place I started to be attracted to the austerity I found in Christian imagery. One day I was feeling so depressed and low that I went into the only Christian shop in town. I thought it was a bit scary in there. I looked for a book about Mary, whom I still felt a reverence for even though I didn't know how to explain it. I found a book about Medjugorje (a site of reported Marian apparitions in Bosnia and Herzegovina) and as I read the words of Mary about fasting I suddenly thought I saw a flash of blue color around me and I heard the words: "You are selfish." I thought "Me, selfish?" and I felt offended, especially given my victim mentality. And the next thought was: "This is the essence of Christianity: self-sacrifice."

There was no way that this second thought came from me. It felt like a grace. I was shown the only way ahead. It was a completely new way for me. The moment came and left me suddenly. Yet, I didn't make any big changes in my life, but the experience certainly made me think. My attraction to holy things increased and my questioning of the pagan ways also increased. I sat down in the local Catholic church and prayed in front of a statue of Jesus. I remember asking in my mind: "But what does the heart with thorns around it mean?" I also asked in prayer for advice about the way ahead as I felt so confused.

The day after I moved into a new house, I had a demonic attack which was a very scary experience. The house was situated literally at the foot of the druid hill that I had been attributing special powers to for so many years. As I moved in there, I experienced something that I believe must have been an incubus or succubus attack. I experienced a dark shade of utter pitch-black darkness moving extremely fast approaching me. It coiled itself around like some sort of cobra snake. I was fighting it with every kind of spiritual trick that I knew but none of my old "friends" (i.e. spiritual practices) could help me. I started reading psalm 23 in my despair. It helped a little.

But the next night I couldn't stop the "black matter" from entering me. It felt like a rape on a soul level, because it entered by a spiritual force I could not match and didn't know how to stop it. It felt like it entered my heart and that it would not leave, making me feel many sick feelings for a long time. The sense of it being a sexual assault happened at the level of my heart emotionally, spiritually and physically. It's hard and very uncomfortable to explain what the experience was like. There was a sense of the demon enjoying itself at my cost but all of this happened in my heart although the physical pain was real. I think it possessed me for a while because after that I had many thoughts that were not my own and they were very vulgar. I also felt as if I had something made of metal inside of me a long time after this.

My computer inexplicably was completely damaged that night; it was useless after that. People who saw me the day after were shocked because I looked so different. A lady, who was deeply into the occult, even asked me whether I had been raped. After this attack my life changed radically for the worse. I didn't understand why this bad thing could happen to me just as I was opening up to Jesus. But I still was caught in my New Age beliefs and I didn't realize that they were evil.

[Note: It is very typical that after a person has been under the sway of demons and then begun to turn toward Jesus and

the Church and thus away from evil, that the demons would now severely attack and torment the person. As long as the person was immersed in evil, the demons would stay in the background.]

The day after this attack I went straight to the local Krishna ashram looking for help. I sat in their temple meditating and I felt that I was transported completely into another place. But I didn't feel sure it was good. I was completely spaced out all the time. I didn't feel like I was myself anymore. It was a terrible feeling of loss. I went to another place of pagan worship and sat there meditating hoping that it would help. What I experienced there was similar. I went into some kind of meditative state where I felt that I went completely into another realm. But it was not a comforting feeling. It was more a feeling of emptiness and further alienation from myself. I went to the people working there to get help from this situation. But all they would say was that these things don't really exist. They didn't believe in demons and demon attacks. They would smudge me with incense, but it didn't help.

I was in touch with so many gurus and so many New Age practices and they have all left their mark. I especially notice it now in prayer as their images come up. I notice their destructive effect and how each New Age book, each practice, each guru, left something toxic in me. They have left something of themselves in my soul which now affects me through bad feelings, tendencies and most of all depression and self-hatred.

I also have all kinds of strange phenomena like motoric movements at the base of my spine from the yoga sect making a lot of noise, which is perceptible to others, plus strange and uncomfortable smells which really disturb and distract me. And since what I will call the incubus attack at the place by the druid hill, I experience a clicking sound which is also audible to others as this "thing" tries repeatedly to push itself into me.

One day I went to a beautiful 11th century church in a bigger town nearby. As I sat down all alone on the church bench and took in the surroundings, I started experiencing the inner lights from the kundalini. I still didn't know that these were evil, but I started getting a bit tired of them. There was no consolation associated with them, only some sort of sense of something supernatural happening to me and maybe a sense of pride connected to that. This time I felt no pride. I kept on praying to God to save me from this hellish state that I was in and all the misery in my life.

Suddenly a deeper light emerged, quite different from the yoga lights. I was sitting with my eyes closed. This light seemed to come from a deeper, truly holy source. I felt that this light asked me for permission to enter, which I gave. Then I was flooded with Christ's love for me. It felt like such a personal love. I perceived that He was a Person in a way I had never experienced before. And that his love for me is deeply personal, like He knew me more deeply than I know myself. He also loved me much more deeply than I loved myself. No one had ever loved me like that.

I also got to "know" him a little bit in this experience. I perceived that there was something spiritually very different about Him than from the other spiritual experiences or other "beings" that I had had. He was someone who had shared my human experience and who had now resurrected. Somehow I perceived this resurrected quality which is unique only to Him. I recognized this on some sort of spiritual, emotional and intuitive level. I realized that what He said about himself is true. He is the Son of God, the Only Begotten One. This deep realization really has no words and has never really left me. It left an imprint on my soul which was life-changing.

[Note: The fruits of this experience were very positive. The truths it revealed were also very positive. It is convincingly a grace from God, and not a demonic ruse, which had a profound life-saving impact on her life.]

I wasn't able to stay in the experience for long because it felt very intense. But the effects of it were remarkable. This kept flooding me many days after. It made me feel so incredibly happy. It was a happiness not of this earth. I would walk in the same roads, doing the groceries in the same shop as before, and this light would just make me feel so incredibly peaceful and happy as never before. I knew that this light belonged to the Kingdom of God.

A door had opened. After this experience I went straight to the library nearby which was just next to the cathedral. I went a lot to this cathedral for the next couple of weeks. In the library I went straight to the Christian section. I found a thick book with Christian prayers from all over the world, from all kinds of denominations. I took this book home with me and had the amazing experience that each time I opened this book and read the prayers I would have a supernatural sense of peace. The difference of this type of supernatural was that it was accompanied by a longing to do what is morally right.

Hence the new word in my vocabulary that had such a magnetic appeal to me, and that I would have scoffed at earlier, "righteousness."

I started to frequent the midday service in the cathedral. I liked being able to just come there, undisturbed, and just take in the beautiful surroundings. Many times I would feel great spiritual consolations come to me during the service. I thought everything was so beautiful and new—the words from the Bible, the beautiful stained glass windows depicting scenes from Mary's life. I simply took in the beauty of Christianity, feeling incredibly grateful for this new birth. I must say—if you are a new ager reading this who is searching for spiritual experiences—there is NOTHING like the spiritual experiences you can get as a Christian. Nothing. They completely renew you, change you, make you fall in love with your Creator.

Even after this, the demons were still pestering me, maybe even more than before. I developed an even deeper and more uncomfortable sensitivity to the demonic. I had a new greater spiritual sensitivity, but since my conversion was so recent I still didn't think there was anything wrong with certain practices such as looking at the yoga sect website and participating in a sort of druid circle on New Year's Eve which was arranged by some yoga teachers and friends of mine. But, I had an awkward feeling.

I had enrolled in a course at a charismatic church and I was starting to frequent their Sunday services. I had gone back to the church where I had had my conversion experience several weeks earlier for my first Christian (Protestant) service ever. I had felt the Holy Spirit's presence strongly while the New Testament was being read aloud there. After the service a woman had come up to me asking if she could pray for me. She later became my first Christian friend. She invited me to come to another church—a non-denominational church. This was where I went for a course. Later I would get help with the demonic problems from one of the ministers there. It didn't solve it, but I got some good advice and their prayers over me certainly did help, especially for a day or two.

But the problems would always come back again, especially as I returned to this town where witchcraft was being practiced by so many people. Working in the cafe there I experienced some extreme things. Once, when I turned around from the coffee machine I looked straight into the eyes of what seemed to be a demon. That is, a man was leaning over the counter, but his eyes were a demon's eyes. I had seen this customer before my conversion but I hadn't noticed anything particular at that time. It was a very uncomfortable experience.

Similarly, a friend of mine was into dragons and witchcraft. She said she was communicating with the dragons. I was starting realize that they were evil spirits. I started to see this incredible darkness in her. Actually at times I could see that her whole eyes were black, not just her iris. She would sometimes say mean things.

These demonic manifestations in other people were sometimes accompanied by terrible smells. Some people would "smell" extra bad. It was quite terrible to work in a restaurant serving people with these afflictions. It was difficult not to talk about these things, which I sometimes did. Some people understood because they had similar experiences themselves, and others, I suspect, just thought I was mad.

My whole world view changed at this time. I realized that the New Age/pagan view of "the universe" was actually another name for idol worship. In Christianity, the universe is a child of God—a brother and a sister to me as we are all God's creation. But it certainly isn't God itself. It might sound innocent to think of it that way, but it's actually very dangerous for one's soul because it isn't true. And there is a reason why it fits in with all new paganism and yoga and other New Age practices. Many of them have this in common—either it's the universe as a deity or it's the Indian tantric view of the universe as "a play of consciousness." The old dance between shiva and shakti. I was slowly starting to understand that believing in the universe as god or goddess was actually breaking the First Commandment.

What was so unique and scary about this time in my life was that I was not only understanding this from a book or philosophically, I was actually experiencing it. The problem was that these ideas were so ingrained in me. How was I supposed to think about the world after this? I continued going to the course at the charismatic church. It was good, because I could ask all the difficult questions and I got some answers. I really got an introduction to the main concepts of Christianity there.

[Note: Now, she had to unlearn all the New Age ideas and spiritualities that she had ingested, and begin to learn the truths taught by Christ and his church.]

This course focused on us all being beloved children of God. It was perfect for me at that time. The leader of the course made me aware of how New Age practices let in lots of demons. I told her about the guru I had (I still thought that she was "good"), but this teacher said that I should stop doing the yoga practices immediately. She said that the guru was just a human being. I remember reacting to that and feeling criticized and judged by her. I thought that she simply didn't understand. But I certainly kept thinking about what she had said.

I had some horrid attacks by the enemy. At the end of one of the really bad attacks, I experienced God's light. Not knowing how to fight something that is purely spiritual and which hates me so much and clearly is much stronger than me and wants to destroy me—I felt at the end of my wits. The help I got at the Charismatic church would only last for a short while. I felt the certainty that this would be a very tough fight, that is, the demons fighting for my soul. But God would win in the end.

[Note: Now that she had seriously begun her Christian journey, the demons would no longer hide but rather attack her directly and fiercely.]

During the months after my conversion, I had been thinking about the Catholic Church. I realized that I had a connection to it—many of my thoughts and preferences were kind of Catholic. Many of the saints had a very strong appeal to me—and the old medieval churches that I visited had many beautiful paintings and stained-glass windows depicting saints which inspired me and helped me on my faith journey. But some of the people around me had very negative thoughts about the Catholic church.

I soon went to talk with the local Catholic parish priest. But I wasn't ready yet to join. I had many misconceptions about the Catholic church both from my New

Age years and from the non-denominational Christians that I was with at the time. I also pondered a lot about the fact that mostly only the Catholic church had monks and nuns and I was wondering why. My conclusion was that it had to have something to do with the sacraments—most of all the Most Blessed Sacrament. It was much more than an intellectual conversion. I felt a very warm connection to the Catholic Church.

I went on retreat at a monastery of Catholic nuns. I had felt an attraction to monastic life for a while and I looked for monasteries online back in my home country as I was planning to move back. I found this monastery which was in a beautiful rural location. I stayed on at the monastery as a volunteer for some months later that year and they put me in contact with Msgr. Rossetti. After meeting him, only then did things start to change for me. Previously, pure faith and prayer had some effect, and also the prayers of the people at the charismatic churches, but afterwards the demons would always come back.

After the first exorcism prayers with Msgr. Rossetti, I felt a change. Actually the day after the session I was just going to have a nap during the day and, as usual, the demons would attack me and not allow me to have a moment's rest. But suddenly I felt this light and spiritual force come right through me and fight the evil that was trying, and had been succeeding, to get inside me. This new spiritual force met the evil just like a sword—like a defensive blow it hit the enemy and managed to stop him. This is the first time I had experienced anything similar. As this happened I "saw" an image spiritually just like the one on the Miraculous medal– and then came also the name and presence of St. Joseph. This is the first time ANYTHING could match and counteract the horrible attacks I was experiencing. I felt a strong sense of hope.

It's not until I started receiving the exorcism prayers that I felt St. Joseph coming to my aid. He steps in like a sort of buffer between me and this terrible dark force. I feel more protected from it. And of course, the Blessed Virgin helps me so much. I put myself under her protection! Blessed be the holy Catholic Church!

Before our exorcism sessions, I was quite nervous, but very quickly I felt safe. But the feelings I had both before, after and during the first session were not good. My heart had the most horrible feelings of dread, pain and malice. I didn't understand where it came from. Later I understood that it was the demons. The demons didn't want me to take part in the sessions and the prayers which made them become more obviously present. At the end of the first session something happened. I felt that something very clearly was "lurking" inside me, and I sensed a disgusting smell. Then I could see my face change into an evil grin as a demon came to the surface.

I could feel or hear the demon say that it was never going to let go of me. I could feel clearly that it was delivering a message to Msgr. Rossetti. His reaction was very reassuring because he didn't look bothered at all by what the demon had said. Personally I felt very scared by this message. Since I experienced a strong demonic manifestation during this first session, it became clear that I needed these deliverance sessions.

Msgr. Rossetti gave me a set of deliverance prayers to pray every day. I had strange reactions when praying them, such as choking and coughing. I started taking catechism instructions to become Catholic and I think the demons must have been very angry about this. I suffered horrible anguish and terror from the demonic presence. The incubus sexual demon also attacked me one morning.

About one-and-a-half years later from the point I started the sessions with Msgr. Rossetti, I formally entered the Catholic church. The demons pestered me horribly during the ceremony. But all in all it was a day of great blessings, even though the enemy wasn't too happy about it. I remember this incredible warmth and blessing during my first Mass as a Catholic. And there were many other wonderful blessings.

I am still somewhat affected by the attacks of the enemy. The improvement is massive though. One of the most important things I learned from Msgr. Rossetti was not to fear the demons and their threats. He said they are all liars and that Jesus will protect us. We must not listen to them or let anything they say affect us.

After I moved into a new home, I actually felt that a demon was trying to kill me! It was as if it was holding an iron fist around my heart. My heart seemed to skip many beats and I thought that I might die. I prayed to Jesus in despair and at this point I really could feel Jesus come and command the demon to leave. The demon had to obey. I think the sessions with Msgr. Rossetti were instrumental in helping me get the courage to ask Jesus for help in a situation like that. Ultimately that is what the exorcism sessions with him are all about—to call on God's help through prayer.

Many of the prayers we prayed were incredibly beautiful. Some of the prayers seem to have more of an effect than others. In the beginning, I was often feeling horrible before and after the sessions. I was "manifest-ing the demons" which needless to say wasn't a very comfortable experience. Some of it was very scary such as feeling "other" eyes over my own eyes. Plus during sessions I experienced very painful stomach aches, in-tense nausea, and feeling completely hopeless, like the darkness was swallowing me.

[Note: A common symptom of being involved in witchcraft, wicca and other forms of divination is an increasing darkness, depression, hopelessness and sometimes inner anger which take a strong hold on the person. It takes much prayer and virtuous living to expunge this darkness.]

It was especially the prayers against the demons of divination that brought forth a lot of demonic reac-tions. Unfortunately, these demons of divination, which are so common in witchcraft and all related practices, are deep-seated and difficult to get rid of. But after two years of prayers I now have very few reactions during the sessions with Msgr. Rossetti because the demons are much weaker. Thus we don't meet so often anymore be-cause it simply isn't necessary.

The demons were literally torturing me. It was hard to see sometimes. I wanted to read the Bible or a book about a saint but I couldn't see properly and the letters were all a blur. This had always accompanied the worst demonic attacks. The inability to see properly—reading was certainly impossible.

Msgr. Rossetti helped me to see which demons were the worst and naming them. This is helpful in getting rid of demons. The yoga sect and the witchcraft demons were bad. Also the "goddess" demon has been hard to get rid of. I still need to reject them on a daily basis. If I'm weak or stressed or something dark is going on around me, I can sense that they are still around me and try to take advantage of my weakness to get in again. But now that I am stronger spiritually I can get rid of them more easily.

I didn't feel so alone after I started praying with Msgr. Rossetti. Suddenly I had someone with me who understood my situation and who could explain it to me. This was so unique and such a gift from God. A couple of months into our meetings we had a session together and clearly many demons left. Msgr. Rossetti said that they were very angry about it. We both experienced that they were attacking us intensely. There was a huge sense of pressure and oppression around me. My vision got unclear and my thoughts got extremely dark and depressive. I also felt very sleepy. I could sense something very dark moving fast around me, pushing in on me.

In fact, I realized that the feelings of depression and anxiety were caused by the demons because these feelings got very intense during this session. And I understood that this was because the demons got angry because I was being prayed over by an exorcist. And suddenly these feelings and sensations lifted, and I felt very happy realizing it wasn't my real way of being. This was an important insight. It had been caused by the demonic. I understood that probably most of the problems of depression that I have had over the years has been caused by the demonic. There was a huge sense of a lift and I actually was smiling and feeling very peaceful. Things got a lot lighter after this.

In the beginning I was basically handicapped by the demons. Both before the sessions but also the whole day long. I couldn't work and I was afraid of meeting people. I was sensitive to other peoples' demons and I never knew what kind of demons they may have with them. I could experience some nasty attacks from them especially if the person was involved in the occult. Now I study full time and I'm less afraid of meeting people even if they do have demons. Msgr. Rossetti explained to me that the demons WANT to keep us isolated. It was when he said this that I realized that my tendency to sit inside all the time and being afraid to walk out and meet people wasn't healthy. In fact, it was demonic.

As our prayer sessions have progressed, deeper psychological issues such as depression, anxiety and some unresolved traumatic experiences from childhood have come up and I realize why the demons had such a hold on me. I have also understood that I have been holding on to very intense anger, rage and unforgiveness towards others and myself. I think demons use psychological wounds in order to get into peoples' psyches and bodies. And the psychological issues worsen. It's a nasty business. But step by step it gets lighter and lighter. Again, prayer and the sacraments, keeping close to God, knowing that we are God's children and deeply loved and wanted by Him is medicine against this.

[Note: Yes, she had an important insight in that demons hang onto our inner anger and unforgiveness. They exploit our inner psychic wounds. Thus, her liberation from the demonic also includes this inner emotional healing and forgiveness.]

I went to group psychotherapy, for two years after my conversion, for treating depression and anxiety. It helped me to see patterns of behavior that have been blocking me in making good choices, such as thinking that others hate me or dislike me, being easily hurt and offended, and taking too much responsibility in group settings. It was at times very painful to be confronted with my own darkness and confusion. Especially realizing how paranoid I could (and still can) be. This was spiritually helpful in addition to being psychologically helpful.

But I also felt the main thing in therapy that was missing, namely Jesus. I think it would have been so much better if we could also have prayed and called on the name of Jesus during group therapy sessions, and talked more about the power of forgiveness. I could see that many of the people in the group also had spiritual issues, but I didn't say anything about it because I didn't consider it to be safe to talk openly about these things in a conventional therapy setting.

Often the demons' feelings are mixed with mine. I might think that it's me who is depressed or confused or angry, but then during the session I realize it's really their feelings. I know this because my depressions are usually a lot better after a session with Msgr. Rossetti. I might feel deeply depressed before the sessions start and then very light and happy at the end of it. This has happened many times, thanks to the "renounce, reject and rebuke prayers" that I learned from Msgr. Rossetti in which I renounce these demonic feelings. The demons now feel more outside me than inside me. And I am now functional even in the morning; I am able to pray and study and think clearly.

[Note: *The emotions of a demonically afflicted person and the demons are intertwined. In the early stages of liberation, the person typically does not realize that much of what they are feeling is coming from the demons. We teach them to "dis-appropriate," that is, to recognize that the evil thoughts and emotions come from the demons and to reject them. In this woman's case, the demons were exacerbating her underlying psychic wounds and depressive affect. One could almost "see" the demons around her eyes and after the exorcism prayers, the demonic depression lifted.*]

One time, I was scheduled to pray with Msgr. Rossetti. Strangely I somehow "forgot" our appointment even though I was home and ready to talk. I am sure that the oppression had something to do with it. My heart hurt a lot, like I have a piece of metal in it, and my thoughts were heavy and negative. When this mood hits me, I am likely to forget what time it is, and fail to get to things on time. Luckily I remembered and we met and prayed together. I got a lot of help. It eased the pain in my heart and my mind got cleared. I realized that I had completely lost hope. I'm upset because I'm not always able to realize that it's demonic when these moods come over me. But the prayers really helped and I am very grateful.

The demons that I felt were pushed out some time ago by Msgr. Stephen's prayers were the ones from eating food offered to Krishna from my past. It's called prasad. It means "gift" in sanscrit, but it certainly is a curse. I remember how "spiritual" the food felt when I ate it. Now I understand how this wasn't a good thing at all. Sometimes I can feel the smell of this "Krishna food" around me. It's associated with spiritual movement around my heart area, like they have put some sort of roots into me. But still, I feel so much better after the sessions.

[Note: Food can indeed be cursed. There is a prayer we use in an exorcism for someone who has ingested a cursed object such as food. This prayer was very effective with her. Typically, one of the ways a witch curses someone is to have the person eat cursed food. A simple blessing over the food is usually enough to lift any curses on one's food. Thus, the time-honored tradition of blessing one's food before a meal is important.]

I have to really take care to not let the demons of depression and hopelessness take hold of me. They are very related to the demons of witchcraft, sorcery and yoga. But they are more difficult to spot sometimes, because they masquerade as my own feelings. These have been very challenging demons for me to get rid of. Unforgiveness and bitterness are also very demonic and I am just realizing how much they have been affecting me. But I am getting better and better at refusing these thoughts and feelings as they come. Going to Mass and confession as often as possible is very important for me in order to keep clear. Praying the rosary and staying close to Mama Mary has also been a key to success for me in vanquishing demons.

Recently, after the session with Msgr. Stephen, I woke up feeling the curses from a pagan priestess, who was a witch, put on me. Terrible. Also, I sensed the smell of something rotten and putrid that I get from the demons of witchcraft. It is pure hatred of human beings. And it's on my heart.

Sometimes certain saints seem to be very close, for example, St. Charbel and St. Gemma Galgani. The prayer and presence of several saints has been very important in the spiritual fight that I have been in. The Latin prayers of exorcism feel very powerful, and I always feel peace or some new insight from it. It feels like heaven and the angels come a little bit closer during the exorcism prayers. In the beginning I used to manifest the demonic a lot during this prayer, but not anymore. The demonic hold on me has lessened greatly. Thank God. I am so grateful for the help that I have received. It has been life-saving and life-changing. God has been very merciful to me.

I still have a fight with the demonic, even after so many years (five) after my conversion (but only two years as a Catholic). But thanks to the prayer sessions with Msgr. Rossetti and with me becoming fully Catholic, I can now actually function again. I sleep well, I study, I work out and I am finally out of a very long period of isolation. I see friends again, and I have forgiven family members so that I can actually meet them and have a good time with them.

More and more I realize that I am a beloved child of God and that discerning His will for me and doing it is what will bring the greatest happiness in my life and in the life of those around me, both in this life and in the life to come. I thank God for his goodness and kindness to me, and that He was willing to forgive me after all the ways I offended Him. Going to confession and receiving the Holy Eucharist at Mass has made my life completely different I am now SO much more free from the demonic. It's incredible. I can have a life again. But it's still a journey....

EPILOGUE

In this person's journey, there are many important insights and learnings. She was deeply involved for years in the New Age and occult, and thus it has taken five years of concentrated prayer and virtuous Catholic sacramental living for her to get her life back. It was a long and difficult struggle but she did so with tenacity and faith, to her great credit. People should not underestimate the evil involved with her former occult practices. Moreover, she had some powerful positive spiritual experiences and graces from God which were key in turning her life around. In the beginning, the demons were mostly hidden and slowly her life became immersed in depression and darkness. But she slowly turned toward the light, thanks be to God. Then the demons no longer hid themselves and started to torment her, as they typically do when someone turns to God. As an exorcist, one of the key points of discernment is how the person functions outside of exorcism sessions. As noted, she got her life back. The demons were destroying her. Now, she has found a sense of life and hope in Jesus. She still is not completely freed so she will need to continue to be particularly vigilant and to engage in deliverance prayers as needed. However, it is such journeys to life which also inspire us who are exorcists and their team members. We rejoice in the Lord when we see someone who was "dead and has come back to life."

Sex With a Witch[24]

BACKGROUND

"JUAN" WAS INVOLVED IN AN ADULTEROUS RELATIONSHIP
WITH A WOMAN "N" WHO TURNED OUT TO BE A PROFI-
CIENT WITCH, UNBEKNOWNST TO HIM. *After some time, he
ended the relationship and returned to his family, hoping to
restore his life to normalcy. However, his former lover, enraged by the breakup, used her dark powers to torment and
curse him.*

*Daily she unleashed a series of curses upon him. Because
of his sinful, sexual intimacy with him, her curses had a special ability to affect him directly and thus anyone with whom
he is intimately connected including his spouse and children.
Thus, N's curses caused Juan severe physical pain and significant financial troubles. The curses affected not only him but
also his family, leading to a cascade of misfortunes and suffering. His daughter suffered inexplicable pains and illnesses.
His wife was tormented, especially in the mind with demonic
obsessions.*

*N was and is intent on breaking up the family and having
Juan return to her. Juan reached out to Msgr. Rossetti who
has been praying with him online regularly now for over three
years (he is distantly located from him). The following are excerpts from Juan's emails and texts to Msgr. Rossetti.*

*[Throughout the narrative, Msgr. Rossetti will make com-
ments to the reader to explain what is happening.]*

Excerpt 1

Hello Msgr Rossetti

After almost 20 years of working for this company, I got involved with a woman "N." Little by little she became involved in my work area and over time I got into an extramarital relationship with her. I know I failed God and my family. I got involved with this woman who was also married. God knows that I prayed and asked God very hard to get rid of it because I felt very bad about what I was doing, I even went to church and confessed to the priest a few times, but it was difficult to separate myself from that relationship.

Eventually my wife began to suspect. She also told me that N attacked her physically outside the house, but I was blind and did not believe her. N finally denounced me at work and I lost my job. My wife found out and I confessed everything to her.

From there, N began to threaten and physically hit my wife. She started sending scores of daily text messages and phone calls from different phone numbers. We blocked her phone number dozens of times to no effect. We changed our own phone numbers over 25 times and she immediately knew the new number, much to our surprise.

We have made reports to the police but nobody believes us. In fact on some occasions my wife herself ends up at risk of being arrested. Everything turns against us in a matter of seconds.

My wife constantly has horrible dreams. Horrible marks and bruises appear on her skin. Suddenly she changes her personality and verbally assaults me in a way that she would never have done in the past. N continues with her threats and messages of highly morbid and threatening content including pornographic images and threats directed at my children.

We sought help from several priests but nobody believed us and even distanced themselves from us. All our friends and acquaintances also turned their backs on us. N sent text messages mocking everything we went through. Inexplicably, she knew in great detail everything that was happening to us.

Finally, we went to a priest who then came to bless our house. This priest listened to us, believed us, and started to offer Masses, and pray for us. But there came a point when this woman just did not stop, and the priest told me that it was all he could do.

In her slew of daily text messages, N makes fun of us and taunts us. She knows exactly where we are, what we are doing, and who we are with. She even knows when my wife is bathing or sleeping. She enters our phone calls and laughs and mocks us.

I am desperate and I really need help in the most urgent way since I fear for the life of my family and mine. I'm completely ignorant about this kind of situation. I never would have believed N could do such things.

I have been praying a lot. The priest mentioned to us that what she is using to know everything about us is a "Monitoring Spirit." I have been looking and praying against that as well but it seems like nothing works. Please if you could help me, I would appreciate it with all my heart.

[Note: Juan and Msgr. Rossetti began praying deliverance prayers live online on a regular basis. Through occult knowledge from demons, N knew when the meetings were scheduled

and barraged Juan with texts before, during and after. When the prayer sessions start, N sends a text and says she and her "deity" are ready for the session. Likely she intensifies her curses at that time to try to nullify the prayers.]

Excerpt 2

How did N find out about our appointment tomorrow? I don't know. As I mentioned before, she knows all what we do, even when our conversation has been only by email. The calls and messages from her do not stop, offensive as always, morbid and threatening. After our last session, my wife was somewhat calm until a few hours ago.

My wife is being attacked more and she is disturbed, at times she changes her mood in a matter of seconds and begins to insult me. Last Saturday she wanted me to leave her on the street and, according to her, she would live in the streets. She said goodbye to the children and they were devastated. Fortunately, by 3:00 am, we managed to convince her, between my eldest son and me, to return home and she returned safely. Again, she reacted in a way which wasn't like her. It was horrible.

The next day, I received many, very long messages from N where she refers to the fact that yesterday was a very heavy day, since what she did made her sweat too much (she is likely referring to the curses she is casting against us). But she called it a successful day.

A couple of hours ago around 1:00 am the dogs began to bark incessantly and woke me up. When I heard the dogs barking and saw that my wife was asleep (which is not common since she is more sensitive to noise than I am), I tried to wake her. But for a few seconds I couldn't wake her up and little by little she opened her eyes, during these seconds she desperately struggled and tried to physically attack what she sees in her sleep. She woke up highly disturbed and she started to cry and got very nervous and sometimes aggressive with me since she blames me for what is happening to her.

This happens to her often, ever since N started harassing us. She says that in her dreams they are attacking her and they want to rape her or they are beating her and she does everything to free herself, or on occasions they harm one of our children. She turned on the light and her leg was red and bruised. This had happened before and marks appeared on her skin.

As she returned to the bedroom, the phones began to ring. N calls and/or sends an infinity of messages mocking what happened. She challenges us saying that there will be no power that can stop her from doing what she has already started. I just continued praying, lit a candle in the image of the Virgin of Guadalupe and the Sacred Heart of Jesus, and continued praying.

We are very concerned because our little daughter is ill, and does not improve. She complains of a headache, stomachache, chills and is losing a lot of weight and hair. They have already done many laboratory studies at the hospital and nothing appears. We began to suspect that N has something to do with this.

Somehow this woman found out that I am in communication with you and she sent messages of mockery and threat. She did this earlier when I told her that finally a priest began to help us with prayers. She scoffed and told us that the priest could not do anything for us and he would end up walking away from us.

The situation is not easy to see my family go through this, but I have faith in God that He will help us to get out of all this.

[Note: The witch's power comes through demons. Bruises and marks on the skin can indeed be caused by demons. They also attack at night through what seems like dreams but in reality are demonic attacks in the mind. Raping and tormenting people are typical demonic mental attacks. Juan's wife's bouts of changing her personality and becoming highly aggressive and accusatory toward him also appear to be demonic. N has a detailed daily knowledge of what their family is doing; this is occult knowledge acquired through demons.]

Excerpt 3

I'm sorry for the late response, I'm trying to convince my wife to meet with you but for some reason she just doesn't want to do it. Sometimes I don't recognize her. In the past, she would be more than happy to meet with a representative of the church without a single question. I'll continue talking with her and I hope I can convince her.

N's attacks continue against us, but mainly against my wife, especially when she is asleep. Texting by N is incessant during the day but at night my wife wakes up totally desperate, screaming and making movements with her hands as if defending herself from something or someone. When she is awake, she tells me that she feels how they physically climb on her and attack her and make fun of her. The day after these attacks my wife has bruises or damage to her legs, even words like DEATH or things like that have appeared on her skin.

Followed by messages from N asking and making fun with questions like: "How are your wife's legs?"

I tried making a report to the police again but now they are no longer accepting them. I have called them repeatedly and they agree that an officer will call me to talk but that never happens. After this, I receive messages from N mocking that the police will never listen to me since she has control over them too.

I am extremely concerned because my daughter continues to be ill with a headache, a stomachache and sometimes she says she loses her sight. They have already performed blood tests and X-rays but nothing comes out. This is getting worse with vomiting and hair loss and the doctors do not find anything wrong with her. My concern is that now N has messed with my daughter and is doing her some harm. N said in one of her previous messages that she would harm my daughter.

As you can see, I am very frustrated and I don't know what to do, since I pray and beg God for help but things have not changed from a year ago.

Excerpt 4

[Note: A sign of N's evil is her persistent rage against Juan and his family. She is bent on destroying the family including the children. She curses and tortures them relentlessly. Such a persistent and consuming obsession with violence and destruction is typical of a demonic rage. I asked Juan if N ever gave him any "food" or anything to eat, wondering if he ate anything cursed from her. Juan responded that she had.]

N volunteered many times to go and pick up food and bring it back for lunch. I remember one particular time she came to my office with a small container and she asked to see my hands and she began applying a cream on my hands. The container she brought wasn't labeled and I remember she told me she prepared that especially for me.

[Note: This "especially made cream" was likely cursed by her. I asked Juan if he had other extra-marital relationships with other women. Juan responded no.]

No, I'm not the kind of person looking for extra-marital sex. I cannot explain myself what happened and why I failed.

This is the very first time I heard the hoot of the owl. I heard the owl and I knew it was there on the back of my property. I think N has something to do with the owl being there. We have never had one before this.

I am having hard time sleeping, I wake up every day around 3am, no matter at what time I go to bed the night before. Today I slept until my alarm went off at 5:00am which was an improvement. Once again, thank you very much for all you do for me and my family.

[Note: I suspect that N may have targeted Juan from the beginning. Clearly she is a high-level witch and in close league with Satan. As such, she would receive "assignments" from him, which might have included destroying Juan and his family. This does not excuse his adulterous actions, for which he does take responsibility, but the entire dynamic seems more than accidental. In fact, Juan said that N initiated the initial contacts including calling him inexplicably at night. Never-

theless, even a high-level witch cannot make someone commit adultery and Juan is responsible for his own actions.]

Excerpt 5

Last Sunday my wife reacted aggressively to me where she kind of lost control. Fortunately, she came back to herself and apologized, and the rest of the day was just fine. I'm really thankful with God because she never came back and apologized for her reactions before.

During the week we received a bunch of messages from N. However, I received a lot less than previous weeks. There was only three or four per day. I know my wife received a lot this week because she ended up turning off her cellphone.

Previously, I didn't believe that all this was possible for a witch and curses. I was even a bit skeptical about it. But seeing the damage that is being done to my daughter, my wife and me, it is clear that people can do a lot of physical damage through it.

Later, in several messages, N mentioned that I would lose one of my feet. She texted that I would be lame and that no one would want to be with me. I started with a small pain in my left foot, this pain worsened, and I decided to go to the podiatrist. They gave me some insoles for my shoes. The pain is now intense to the point that it is difficult to finish my workday. The most curious thing is that the doctor took X-rays and he did not find anything wrong with my foot.

My daughter started complaining a lot again last night about headaches and pain on her legs. This morning she didn't want to go to school because of the pain and that's unusual because she loves school and she is an excellent student. It seems like N came back again just to continue harassing us.

How difficult it is to understand how people can have so much hate in their hearts that they live only to hate. That has to be full possession of evil over those people. That's the only way I can understand that.

[Note: It is stunning the persistence of N and her evil curses against the family. For over three years, she curses them daily; sends countless texts; and monitors their activities. She is consumed with destroying Juan and his family, even while professing that she and Juan are "meant" to be together as a couple always.]

Excerpt 6

I will call it a heavy week—so many text messages from N. My wife went back into that attitude that I mentioned to you before where she just wants to fight and argue with me. Not even a minute after my wife and I have an argument, I receive a bunch of messages from N talking about the situation that my wife and I just argued. It is as if she is listening to us all the time.

I feel tired and hopeless. I have no more power and energy to keep moving. It has been three years fighting and I just feel like there is no exit to this. Not sure what to do or how to do it. I am sorry to bother you and I'm sure I sound like baby, but I'm just super frustrated and tired.

My little one woke up in the middle of the night crying because "someone was in the room and woke her up." She continues to complain about her sickness.

I'm praying every day. I have faith in God that this situation will stop. It is just so hard sometimes to see all this happening with the feeling I can't do anything to stop it. I wish this email was to give you better news, but this is where we are.

[Note: It is also likely that N is affecting Juan's thinking too. In addition, to making his wife unusually aggressive and distrusting, she is affecting his mind with hopelessness, doubt and discouragement, even despair. This is typical of demonic influence on the mind, i.e., demon brain.]

Excerpt 7

My wife is more calm. We started praying the rosary again together. N was still sending text messages and calling my wife as usual.

Saturday I was so happy because N didn't send any messages. I was really optimistic, but Sunday she sent messages all day long. She went back to her normal making comments with specific details of what my wife and I do as a couple. I am not sure how she can see what we do no matter at what time of the day it is. It feels like someone is right next to us at all the times watching us. She sometimes actually sends photos of us, as if she was in the room and taking our picture.

During one of the first of the prayer sessions you and I had, I felt a sensation or need to vomit. I ignored it and I thought it was just a coincidence, but this last session I really felt like I was ready to throw up. I'm wondering if this is part of it, or just my imagination?

I want to thank you again for all your time and effort. My wife and I are desperate, and we would like to see the difference right away. But I really believe that God is in control and this situation would be a lot worse if God was not protecting us.

[Note: In each prayer session, Juan will spend a few moments with the dry heaves. He tries to vomit something up but nothing comes up. However, I view this as a positive sign that the prayers are working and the evil is slowly being ejected. He particularly reacts to the prayers for those who have ingested cursed objects, which he undoubtedly has. Certainly N gave him many such cursed foods during their one year relationship before he broke it off.]

Excerpt 8

As soon as we finished the session today, I saw that I had received a couple of messages from N where she said the following: "My love, I'm ready to be on the session to pray. I haven't contacted you because I was getting ready to be with you praying. Did you miss me? I would never forget about you. You will live with me for the rest of your life. You will never get rid of me, no matter if the Father wants or not. That will never occur."

I got a second text: "Please don't vomit. I'm here with you. You know my success is coming soon. Don't go vomiting, you are not alone."

Excerpt 9

My wife has been in bad mood the whole week and we barely speak. For whatever reason, when I approach her she just get upsets.

Yesterday my wife had to go to the school to pick up some paperwork and N showed up. She was very upset about it and started arguing with me. I insisted asking what happened but she just got more upset, especially when I mentioned to her that I will call the police and I will hire a lawyer. She just exploded right there and she told me if I do that she will declare against me. She will deny all what is happening because if I call the police the kids are at high risk from N.

By the end of the day my wife approached me and said, "Look what this crazy woman is capable of! She removed the sunglasses and her eyes and face were super red. N intercepted her outside the school and threw something on her eyes and threatened her. If I tell other people what happened, N said she will cause damage to our kids.

My wife is terrified of N causing harm to our kids and she told me that if I call the police or hire a lawyer she will leave home and she will declare all against me. I filed many reports online, but I had to cancel with the officer.

I don't know what else to do. I really believe God will help us, but sometimes my faith goes down especially when I see the damage caused to my kids.

[Note: Fear and anger fuels demons and curses. N intentionally torments them, especially Juan's wife, to instill fear. Threatening one's children is a common demonic tactic. This fear and family discord help to fuel the curses and it strengthens the demons' hold.]

Excerpt 10

I haven't received a single message from N since a week after our last session, about 4 weeks ago. I got a feeling that now she is planning something different. My daughter has been ok with some "sickness" here and there but nothing that puts her in bed. She has headaches really often.

My wife and I are doing well; there are not that many fights between us. She has been sleeping in the living area for the last year and obviously there is no intimacy between us. But at least the kids do not see us fighting or offending each other.

There are a lot of health issues for me. The pain in my foot is getting worse and worse. Now I am pre-diabetic. I quit drinking soda but my glucose numbers are still going up. I am feeling a lot of sadness or depression. Sometimes I just can't find a reason to continue moving forward. Economically, no matter what I do or how many hours overtime I work, there is ALWAYS an unexpected situation that doesn't allow me to keep a single penny.

It seems like everything was quiet for few days but I kind of feel this sensation as if someone was looking at me, but I ignore it. Physically I'm having a really hard time. Pains in my foot, my back, my elbow—I'm actually having an appointment with the specialist again tomorrow Wednesday to see if I should have surgery on my foot. Two weeks from now I have another appointment with specialist for my elbow.

Excerpt 11

This is crazy but today for our online meeting, I cannot login. It's the same laptop and wi-fi that I have always been using for a long time. But now, I cannot find my wi-fi network even though all of my neighbors' networks are listed. The only wi-fi I cannot see is my own.

There is a saying that: "Tell me what you brag about, and I'll tell you what you lack." Since this evil started, N is always texting: "HA, HA, HA, HA, HA" or emojis with happy faces or laughing, perhaps to hide what is really happening in her life. She says she is happy and successful and she needs to really show it to me. Not sure why? When someone is happy it's absolutely easy to detect, it's actually contagious sometimes. But when you have to force it on others so the others can buy what you are trying to sell… I can feel from her some kind of miserable life—alone? abused? sadness?

I really thought she disappeared from our lives finally but, as I mentioned, I was afraid that she was only using a different tactic. Last Saturday night while I was sleeping, I felt someone touching me. I can remember trying to wake up but I couldn't, until finally this hand grabbed me really hard on my masculine member and I woke up abruptly. Somehow N's face came to my mind. I thought it was just a bad dream but it was so real. The next day I could still feel a little pain and sensation where she grabbed me.

Last night, the car alarms went off so many times and more messages arrived again from N. Here is some of her messages (with bad words crossed out):

Ha ha. So what do you think??? That's right, son of a CHEAP ADULTERESS XXXXX XXXX, that is, your DAMN and disgusting XXXX, daughter of his XXXXX XXXXXX MOTHER, that is, you know. NOTHING AND NOBODY can SEPARATE US.

Until death do us part. I'll be here for the rest of your existence.

How have these weeks been? I am succeeding as always. I am very proud of myself. All achievements. And it is a pride. As a woman I am a WOMAN. AS A PROFESSIONAL I AM.

WHAT MORE CAN I ASK FROM LIFE. 😄😄😄 😄😄😄😄😄😄*. We will be close sooner...* 😉😋😉 *Happy, Happy, Happy*

Father, I feel really desperate, and I just want to quit and disappear and forget about everything... I feel like I have no more energy to fight and continue. I need help and I don't know what else to do but pray.

[Note: N professes that she and Juan will be together and professes some sort of love for Juan, but in reality she is torturing him. In these texts, you can see how angry she is to the point of being irrational and distorting what is happening.]

Excerpt 12

I recognized my failure to God and my family. Recognizing my failure is the only way to realize how much damage I did to the ones I love, damage that might never be repaired. More important I failed God, that's hard to live with, after all He did for us.

I just found this object inside of one of the cars that I don't really use that often. I went to pick up some groceries and once I opened the car it was inside.

[Note: there was black ribbon knotted around his steering wheel with a small figure of a person in it. It was inside his

locked car inside his locked garage. A proficient witch, with the use of demons, can materialize such a thing inside a locked car. The knotted ribbon around the human-like figurine was spell designed to strengthen the evil bond between Juan and N. On another occasion, Juan opened a sealed Amazon package that he ordered and, in addition to what he ordered, was also a note from N. Again, she was able to materialize, through the agency of demons, a note inside a sealed package sent from Amazon.]

Yesterday after the online session, everything started changing. My wife began getting mad and looking for little things to get into an argument. By the end of the day it got worse and we had a fight. Alarms on the cars when off several times and bunch of messages from N congratulating me because of my argument with my wife and her asking not to have sexual intimacy with me.

Unfortunately, my wife believes everything N tells her. This morning she was really upset and angry, and started telling that I'm in cahoots with N and working with her to cause damage to her. N sent her a bunch of messages and some pictures about me having been with her but it never, never happened. I was not with N and haven't been since we broke up some years ago. My wife believes N and thinks I am lying to you just because N sent her some pictures. According to my wife, N and I are together in the pictures.

Also, my daughter was complaining a lot yesterday during the evening and it got worse during the night. I woke up very anxious and afraid of who knows what. I just don't feel good at all. I prayed during the way to work and I felt a little better.

By the way, there is ANOTHER owl around my property making weird noises.

Excerpt 13

Just an update: I received a text message from N with a picture of my wife in her car, as if N was in the backseat and took the picture. My daughter complained all day yesterday and during the whole night about the feeling of "somebody punching her in the stomach."

Before our prayer session, N sent me a text: "I am ready for the prayer session and my god is too." She always knows when we are going to meet and mysteriously is listening in on our conversations.

This has been a very active week for N. More messages than usual, with emphasis about the physical damage that she has been causing to my wife and making fun of it. Other messages make references to "sexual encounters that we supposedly have" and copies are sent to my wife. I have had NO contact with N at all through all of this.

Not sure if the full moon has something to do with these kind of activities but I have noticed that with the full moon the activities increase. Coincidence? I don't know.

Weird dreams happened this week to me and I'm just tired. But it is clear that I need to continue and I will. I need to fight for my kids and I need to keep moving forward, no matter how hard the road is. Thank you very much from the bottom of my heart for everything.

A Text From N to Juan

I would have liked you to finally spend thanksgiving with your babies and your wife. But for not doing what you have been

*promising for years—that you are going to leave the disgust-
ing unfaithful witch [referring to his wife] and the parasites
[his children] it was not possible. It is time NOW that you
make up your mind and don't waste any more time without
your babies that need you so much. Either way I hope you have
a good time that it is not a hell like the one you live every day.
This message is special to see if you finally understand that
we were born to always be together and that NOTHING and
NOBODY will be able to separate us. Happy thanksgiving!!*

*[Note: This is a typical bizarre text from N to Juan. N accuses
his wife of being an unfaithful witch although it is N who is
such. Also, N is demanding Juan leave his wife and children
now to be with her or she will punish him. And then she wishes him a "happy thanksgiving."]*

Excerpt 14

Just to give you heads up. Things are going back to bad…
My wife was a little more tolerant during the last two
weeks, but yesterday you can tell something came back
again and she started getting upset again. Last Friday a
voice in my ear woke me up in the middle of the night
mentioning my name. When I woke up I thought it was
just a dream but after a few minutes I started feeling a
weird and uncomfortable sensation as if someone was
right next to me. Yesterday N sent a massive number of
obscene, vulgar messages to my wife and me. Around
7-8 pm the car alarms all went off.

I know I need to trust in God. Believe me every night
as soon as I wake up even for few minutes I pray, if I'm
driving to work I'm praying, or listening to the rosary
in the truck. If I'm literally in the bathroom I'm praying

but it seems like nothing works... I'm desperate, two years already from this crazy Lady. You have been helping me and sometimes there are a little breaks but then the storm comes back again.

I have a horrible sensation wanting to vomit every time we pray, and I'm anxiously waiting to see if something comes out and hopefully this nightmare stops but nothing happens.

I guess today is just not a good day and I need to release a little bit from my load... but I just don't know what else to do. Thanks for all your help and your prayers from my heart.

Excerpt 15

Everything has been quiet; only a couple of messages per day or so. But this is what I found on the bed of my service truck this morning. I'll get rid of it on the road.

[Note: Juan sent a photo. My response to Juan: "It looks like a dead chicken. That would typically be used in occult practices. Throw some holy water on it and on the truck. Don't touch it with your bare hands."]

Excerpt 16

I hadn't even left the driveway at home on the way to Mass and N sent 5 messages to me and my wife. N said to my wife that N and I were going to meet at some point on the road in order to go together to Mass and to have sex. Of course, this was all said with a super vulgar and nasty vocabulary that she always does.

I didn't mention to anyone at home that I was going to church. I didn't mention where I was or where I was going, but N already knew where I was heading even before I pulled out from my house driveway. Sometimes my wife believes these lies from N.

I asked God this morning for protection, peace at home.

Excerpt 17

For some weird reason I haven't received a single message during the last three weeks. I know my wife has but I can't tell how often. Physically I'm not doing that good. I have new pains that appeared for no reason and my legs are killing me. My daughter is complaining about headaches for the last two weeks, but not to the point that she goes to bed anymore.

But after our last session, evil became really active. The pain on my foot is really bad and the pain in my back came back. The pain in my foot is super painful. I'm planning to look for medical assistance because it is really hard and painful to work. But I'm afraid that I just going to waste my money. Last night dogs were barking/crying really weird.

God bless you.

Excerpt 18

Everything is back. Two or three messages per day. Making fun about the pain that I'm feeling in my legs and in my back. N is celebrating because, according to her, I'm getting to the point where I'll be losing the ability to walk. N is harassing me and threatening more pain is coming. My arguing with my wife is back.

It's been almost three years on this and I'm really tired, depressed and losing the faith. It's like God is not listening to my prayers. I screwed up; I failed. I sinned against God. But He knows I was a good man before that for years, always working and attending to my family.

I'm just desperate and with low energy and feeling alone. Please include me in your prayers and ask God for my forgiveness.

I was traveling and while lying on the bed in a hotel, I started having the sensation that someone was here with me, and I noticed something moved by the entrance of the room. I was actually able to see the shadow and how the shadow blocked the light at the entrance. A few minutes after I saw it again a couple of times.

After that, I received a couple of messages from N with a couple of short videos of me showing that she is observing me. They were videos of me in the room, but she was NOT in the room with me and it is inexplicable how she took them. Not even with thousands of miles away from N will she stop harassing me and doing all the satanic things that she does. It's crazy.

[NB: N is what we call a trafficking witch. Through the power of Satan, she can project herself to another place. There is a prayer to nullify a trafficking witch's demonic power on our app/website. Our deliverance prayers are slowly helping Juan and his family. However, the sin of adultery is very grave. Moreover, he did so with a proficient witch which gives her power to inflict serious harm on him and his family. Moreover, his wife will not practice the faith; she is terrified of N; and is unreconciled with her husband. The anger, fear, lack of faith, and unforgiveness fuel the demonic and the witch's curses. Nevertheless, slowly progress is being made and N's ability to inflict damage on the family is being attenuated.]

Excerpt 19

I am OK. The pain in my back came back recently. It really hurts but at least the communication between my wife and me is a lot better. My daughter is ok physically, but it seems like she is having some conflicts with other students at school who are bullying her for no reason. They are students that she doesn't even know. Is N inciting them?

During the rest of the day after we met yesterday, the back pain was reduced considerably. It didn't disappear completely, but for sure I was able to do my job more comfortably.

Excerpt 20

Intense activity last night. My wife and I got into a big fight. It felt like the earlier time when we didn't do anything other than fight and argue. After that my wife received A LOT of messages from N. I didn't receive a single one.

The alarm on one of the cars went off all night until 12:00pm every minute or less. And once again at 3:00am. I noticed that I didn't feel scared when all the activity happened. I actually went to the car and I guess I was hoping to see or face something. But I felt fearless...

Today, the kids don't want to see me and they are all against me again. Once again I feel like we are starting all over again. Honestly I don't want to continue. I'm tired and I feel like there is no reason to continue. Please keep me in your prayers.

I always carry a rosary hanging from the center mirror of my truck. Tuesday morning I found it broken and lying on the floor when I opened my truck to go to work. I hung a new rosary in its place. I thought to let you know about it.

I have an ugly impulse to get in contact with a witch guy that is on the radio that the guys I'm working with are listening to. It seems so real that he is helping people. Three years ago I told you I will not do such a thing and that's what holding me back. I don't want to fail anymore, but I'm desperate.

Excerpt 21

This is crazy: while driving a big bird came out from a field and crashed into the hood of my truck. I pulled over and looked for the bird but couldn't see it. It seemed to have disappeared. I'm not sure but I believe it was an owl.

[Note: Owls are sometines thought to be "familiars" of witches.]

N seems to have this thing with birds. They followed me even inside the store, I remember being inside Home Depot and this bird was right at front of me for a while. I went over to another section and it was there. I thought I was crazy. So many things going on.

After I did my prayers tonight around midnight, under my pillows I found this thing. I don't know what it is. But with closer attention, I noticed that this was not something I put there, or something familiar. I put holy water on it and on my hands and I threw it in the toilet and flushed. I thought it was important to let you know about this.

[Note: Juan sent a photo. It was a small figure of a head about two inches high with a black ribbon knotted around it. This is sometimes called a fortuna or factura and it is type of malefice—casting of an evil spell. Obviously, N materialized it, through the power of demons, under his head. It is a spell to bind Juan to her more closely. As the prayers continue, N wants to maintain the bond so she has to continue to cast spells since the prayers weaken the bond.]

Excerpt 22

I'm not scared and God is with me, and somehow that has been helping me. This evil lady has been kind of quiet, only a couple of messages here and there. Last week she sent almost one per day but other than that not as many as she used to. She continues repeating that I'm going to be losing one of my legs, if you remember she mentioned that for long time.

Lately my foot hurts considerably and I had been using massages and applying different things hoping to get better, but nothing works. I'm feeling ok emotionally. Every time I get this depression and or nervous feeling I just pray and I invoke Saint Padre Pio and Saint Michael the Archangel. My foot does hurts but before I go to sleep I put the rosary over my foot and pray. It feels better sometimes in the morning. I really believe God has heard our prayers and eventually she will be totally out of our life.

What is really, really BAD is our finances at home. Doesn't matter how many hours I work or what I do, we are always short on payments…. No matter what. For example, I put $450 in my lunch box. Well, today when I arrived home N sent us a picture of my lunch box. When I saw the picture I checked the lunch box which was inside my work truck and the money was not there. In place of the money was another black ribbon tied with a knot. Obviously this is a spell from N. Then car alarms started going off on two of the cars several times. Not sure if I want to blame all of what happens to me to witchcraft.

The relation between my wife and I is better, even when we have no intimacy, we can communicate a lot better. My daughter is doing a lot better. I haven't heard her complaining as she used to.

I received an ugly text from N. All kinds of evil comments. She actually mentioned again I'll be losing my foot and I'll never walk again. She just continues sending texts. I got like 15 today.

I can tell N wasn't happy because I prayed with you yesterday. As you know, I received a bunch of messages from her after we met online yesterday. Also, I received a bunch before as well. That you for meeting with me yesterday, thank you for the deliverance session.

Excerpt 23

My daughter seems to be doing better. She complains once in a while but I can tell she is more active. The pain in my leg got worse. I went back to the specialist and they want to do surgery on both feet but I'm not sure about that. A lot of pain in my back on the right upper side and I have felt a horrible nausea for a week. It seems like things are just going a little better. I haven't felt any nausea since you prayed over me yesterday.

[Note: We scheduled a session to pray over him, especially his foot. By the end of the session, the pain in his foot had completely disappeared so we concluded it was a result of a curse. Juan then cancelled the foot surgery.]

Excerpt 24

N didn't send more messages for few days until today. I developed an elbow pain. The pain is getting worse and I thought with ice the pain would go away.

Today N texted me the following comments (I put an X to delete awful words):

hahaha how's your little rotten arm going? 😬😬😬😬
😬😬😬😬😬😬 *you'll be lame in the future. hahaha son of your xxxxxxx mother hahaha the xxxxx*

You will lose your leg hahaha son of you xxxxxxxx. mother hahaha hahaha the xxxxxxx

You know I NEVER lose. Imagine what's coming😲😲

I didn't mention to you about my elbow because I didn't want to relate everything that happens to us with her witchcraft. But it seems like she was behind this as well…

There is another owl on my property.

Excerpt 25

Overall I'm doing ok. I haven't received a single message from N since the last time we prayed. I think she is still harassing my wife but it seems like not that often.

The relationship between us is better; we can communicate and spend some time together without it ending with a fight. We are living together but that's it. There is not an actual marriage relation between us. But at least the kids are not seeing episodes of insults and fights.

I haven't received any text messages from N anymore, but some weird things happen around like things falling down by themselves, weird noises, knocking on the wall of my bedroom ... and another owl in the property.

Just to let you know that the pain in my foot is maybe only 30% of what it was during the last few days. Pain in the back is still really painful. Thanks again for all your prayers and help.

[Note: It is obvious that these owls appearing on his property are not all the same owl because he admitted that he shot 3 or 4 of a total of about 5 that he saw on his property.]

EPILOGUE

Msgr. Rossetti and Juan are meeting less frequently. The demonic obsessions affecting his wife and the physical ailments affecting his daughter have subsided. There are fewer texts and emails from N. However, she is still cursing him and the effects are now mainly found in physical ailments affecting Juan such as a pain in the back or foot. The other kinds of symptoms such as car alarms going off and similar physical manifestations have subsided. It appears that the deliverance prayers have blunted the effects of N's witchcraft. As the impact of her curses and spells declines, it is to be expected that Juan's family members would be less affected and the primary portal to the demonic, i.e. Juan, would be the last to suffer the effects. This is a sign that the curses are less and less effective. However, the wife continues to be estranged from her husband and remains frightened of N and does not practice the faith. This residual anger, unforgiveness, lack of faith, and fear fuels the curses and the presence of the demonic and limits the full effectiveness of the prayers.

Deliverance Prayers
for
Laypersons to Use

BELOW ARE SOME OFTEN-REQUESTED DELIVERANCE PRAYERS FOR THE LAITY. These and more such prayers are found on our website: www.catholicexorcism.org and also in our app: "Catholic Exorcism." Deliverance and exorcism prayers can also be found at www.amoe. ph which are provided by our friends in the exorcism ministry in the Philippines.

Also, St. Michael Center for Spiritual Renewal offers a free monthly online deliverance session. For information and registration, go to its website: www.catholicexorcism.org.

BEFORE YOU SAY THESE PRAYERS

Guidelines for Deliverance Prayers for the Laity

1) *These prayers are for use by the laity.*

2) *The prayers in this section are typically phrased to be used for praying over oneself. All individuals have authority over their own selves and bodies and thus they are free to use both imperative prayers (directly commanding demons to leave) and deprecatory prayers (prayers directed to God to cast out the demons) over themselves.*

3) *In accordance with natural law, in addition to having authority over their own selves, they also have authority over their spouses and their children who are still minors. In these cases, they have the authority to use imperative prayers.*

4) *In the case of praying these prayers for others who are not under their direct authority, we recommend the faithful adjust the prayers so that they are directed to God, thus making it a deprecatory prayer. For their own pastoral protection, we recommend that faithful not use imperative*

prayers, *i.e., directly commanding demons to leave, over others whom they do not have authority. Moreover, if an individual is truly possessed by demons, we recommend such individuals be referred to a priest-exorcist appointed by his bishop.*

5) *The common St. Michael prayer, Litany of the Saints, Litany of Loreto, the holy Rosary, prayers to the Sacred Heart and other such traditional Catholic prayers are very efficacious in deliverance praying. These can be found on our app and website under "Prayers for Those Assisting Priests in Exorcisms & Deliverance Praying" or by searching the internet.*

PERIMETER PROTECTION PRAYER

Heavenly Father, I ask that You establish a perimeter of protection around myself (and N.), immersing all of us, our loved ones, our associates, our property, possessions, resources and all in our lives that is provided by Your paternal goodness. I further ask Heavenly Father through the intercession of the Blessed Virgin Mary and Saint Michael the Archangel that You would send Your angels and saints to stand guard over us, our works, our ministries, and all that is done in the Name of Your Beloved Son, preserving us from all evil influence and demonic retaliation, including any and all curses and occult actions sent against us. I especially ask that You preserve us from all that we may be especially susceptible to in our lives, barring the demons or any of Satan's minions from harming or harassing us in any way, rendering them all spiritually deaf, dumb, blind and completely powerless. I ask that You disempower and remove all evil influences that seek to empower, aid, or strengthen the demons or their minions seeking to harm us. I further ask that You grant an abundance of blessings to us, our family members near and far, our priests, and all our loved ones. We ask all this in the Name of Jesus Your Beloved Son, trusting in His Divine Mercy, and through the intercession of His Most Blessed Mother. Amen. [SMC staff]

UMBRELLINO PRAYER FOR TECHNOLOGY

Lord Jesus Christ, Sovereign King enthroned in Heaven, in your love and mercy establish a perimeter of protection with Your Precious Blood around our communication devices and all technology used during this session. Cleanse them with your precious blood and drive from them any satanic influence. Establish around them a sanctuary of your mercy where Satan and any other evil spirit or human agency cannot interfere. I ask Father that you would block, bind, rebuke and render impotent any assault of the evil one from them in any way. Father, we ask you to allow them to enjoy the protection of the Blessed Mother, St. Michael the Archangel, and all the Holy Angels. We ask for the special intercession of Blessed Carlo Acutis. We ask this in Your Most Holy Name. R. Amen. [SMC staff]

AGAINST SPIRITS OF RETALIATION

Lord Jesus Christ, in your love and mercy, pour Thy Precious Blood over (I) your servant N. so that no demon, disembodied spirit, or evil power may retaliate against me (him/her). O Blessed Mother of God, Most Immaculate Virgin Mary, our mother and queen, surround me (him/her) with thy mantle, blocking any retaliating spirits from having any authority over me (him/her). St. Joseph, protector of the Holy Family and God's Holy Church, Terror of Demons, protect us from the attacking enemy. St. Michael, our defender, surround us with thy shield, and with your flaming sword punish severely the wicked spirits, so that no spirit may take revenge on us. My Holy Guardian Angel (Holy Guardian Angel of N.) defend this your ward. St./Sts. NN. intercede on behalf of N. Queen of Heaven, St. Joseph, and St. Michael, send down the legions of angels under your command to fight off any degenerate spirits that would seek to harm us. All you saints of heaven, impede any retaliating spirit from influencing us. Lord, Thou art the Just Judge, the Avenger of the Wicked, the Advocate of the Just, we beg in Thy mercy, that all we ask of the Blessed Virgin Mary, St. Joseph, St. Michael, and all the holy angels and the saints of heaven in our behalf (and in behalf of your servant N.), be also granted to all our loved ones, those who pray for us and their loved ones, that for Thy Glory's sake, we may enjoy Thy perfect protection. Amen. [see www.amoe.ph]

AN ACT OF FORGIVENESS

(Note: Forgiveness does not mean that what the person did to harm someone was okay. It also does not mean the one hurt should have "warm feelings" about the other person. Rather, it is an act of the will to let go of the hurt and to will the good of the other. Demons feed off unforgiveness. Unforgiveness can dysfunctionally bond the person to the abuser and the one harmed can remain a perpetual victim, under the control of the abuser. Forgiveness allows the person to let go of the harm, to be open to God's healing, and to be set free.)

In the name of Jesus Christ, I willingly forgive anyone who has hurt or harmed me (including N., N., N., etc...).

I forgive them from the bottom of my heart and I ask God to bless them. [3X]

I willingly forgive myself. I renounce the evil spirit of self-hatred. I accept God's forgiveness. And I ask God to bless me. [3X]
[SMC staff]

PRAYER TO BREAK UNHOLY TIES

This prayer is used when the victim has had a long-standing relationship with person(s) involved with the occult or has communicated with "imaginary friends," spirit guides, ascended masters, "elementals," "wandering souls," etc.

In the Name of Jesus, I break any unholy ties, links, and bondages between myself and X and all evil sources and spirits. [3X]

And I command all spirits affecting me associated with these unholy ties, links, and bondages to go immediately and directly to the foot of the cross.

O Most Holy Spirit, enter into the empty spaces left by these spirits and fill me with your presence, love, and protection. Please do not allow these spirits to return.

[Fr. Winston Cabading, "Catholic Handbook of Prayers for Spiritual Liberation and Exorcisms With Redactor's Notes," 1st ed., The University of Santo Tomas Publishing House, Manila, Philippines, 2016, pp. 41,43]

BREAKING CURSES OF THE OCCULT

I ask + Jesus Christ to break all curses and spells sent against me or any of my loved ones or any of our possessions. [3X]

And I ask + Jesus Christ to cast out all evil spirits associated with these curses and spells and to send them immediately and directly to the foot of his cross.

or

In the name of the Lord Jesus + Christ of Nazareth, I ask + Jesus Christ to cast out all spells, hexes, curses, voodoo practices, witchcraft, satanic rituals, incantations, evil wishes, fasting prayers, or any occult action not of the Lord, that have been sent my way or against my loved ones or possessions or have passed down the generational bloodline. I ask + Jesus Christ to command that they be cast out and replaced with a blessing. May the Lord Jesus pour out his precious blood over all aspects of my life and relationships, and I ask him to wash away and cleanse us from all impurities, in his holy name. Amen.

[adapted from Fr. Winston Cabading, "Catholic Handbook of Prayers for Spiritual Liberation and Exorcisms With Redactor's Notes," 1st ed., The University of Santo Tomas Publishing House, Manila, Philippines, 2016, pp. 40-41]

CASTING OUT EVIL SPIRITS OF DIVINATION

Heavenly Father, in the name of your only begotten Son, Jesus + Christ, I denounce Satan and all his works, witchcraft, the use of divination, the use of the Occult Third Eye and the Evil Eye, the practicing of sorcery, dealings with mediums and spiritualists, Ouija boards, astrology, horoscopes, numerology, all types of fortune telling, tarot cards, palm readings, tea-leaves reading, levitation, astral projection, and anything associated with the occult and Satan, whether knowingly or through ignorance, I denounce all of them in the name of the Lord Jesus + Christ who came in the flesh, and by the power of His Cross, His Blood and His resurrection, I break their hold over me.

I confess all these sins before you and ask you to cleanse and forgive me. I confess with my lips and my heart that Jesus Christ is the only Son of God, and ask you Lord Jesus to enter my heart and create in me the kind of person you have intended me to be. I ask you to send forth Your Holy Spirit and renew me with His life-giving and sanctifying gifts, just as when you breathed on the apostles the Holy Spirit after your resurrection and sealed and empowered them on the day of Pentecost.

O God + absolve, remit, and pardon my voluntary and involuntary sins, in word and deed, known and unknown, by day and by night, in mind and thought; forgive me, in Your goodness and love for mankind.

[I renounce all the spirits of divination and the power of demons that came in me to give me this power and I command you to leave me now in the name of Jesus + Christ (3x).]

All spirits of darkness and divination leave me now in the name of Jesus. [*To be repeated by the Afflicted as long as necessary.*]

[adapted from Fr. Winston Cabading, "Catholic Handbook of Prayers for Spiritual Liberation and Exorcisms With Redactor's Notes," 2nd ed., The University of Santo Tomas Publishing House, Manila, Philippines, 2024, pp. 100-107.]

A PRAYER AGAINST TRAFFICKING WITCHES

In the Holy Name of Jesus, I remove all trafficking witches and evil spirits affecting me or my family. May God's defending angels strip these witches and all Satan's minions of psychic powers, demonic and occult powers. May God strip them of all magic charms, psychic vision, curses, and powers of divination. May all their powers and devices be destroyed and cast into the abyss. I ask the Lord to bring these people before His throne and bless them with the revelation of who Our Lord is and His love and plans of salvation for them. Show them how they are being deceived by Satan. I ask the Lord to establish an impenetrable shield of protection between me and my family, and all trafficking witches and their demons. In Jesus' name, I render all trafficking witches and Satan's minions affecting me and my family spiritually powerless. I bind all evil spirits involved and render them deaf dumb and blind. In

Jesus' name, I cast them out. In his Holy Name, I cast them all out. Amen.

[Based on "Prayer Against Trafficking Witches" by Valentine Publishing House. Reprinted with permission. All Rights Reserved. www.catholicdeliverance.com]

PRAYER TO REMOVE GENERATIONAL SPIRITS

Lord Jesus Christ, I ask in Your Most Holy Name to remove any evil spirits that may be affecting my generational bloodline. If any curse or malefice has been introduced by a member of this family, or from outside the family, I ask that you cast it out and cleanse us with Your Most Precious Blood. I willingly forgive my ancestors or any others who are at fault and I ask you to absolve them of this sin and bless them. I repent of any evil that I have done to introduce evil into our generational line and ask for your forgiveness. I particularly pray that you would cleanse our generational bloodline of all curses, illnesses, sicknesses, addictions, financial curses, divorces, abuse, [*here add any evil that persists in your generational bloodline*] and all evils persisting in our generational line. May Your Precious Blood wash over us and cleanse us all. May these evils end now, through your infinite mercy and the power of your Holy Cross. [SMC staff]

A PRAYER AGAINST FINANCIAL CURSES & CONSECRATION OF GOODS TO THE BVM

I invoke my natural law rights over my own property and finances. I lift any curses sent against me or my property or finances. I reject any sins that may have led to these curses coming against me and ask for God's forgiveness. I break any unholy bonds that allowed such curses to come upon me. I command the demons related to these curses to leave permanently and not be replaced by any other evil spirits. I ask the Blessed Virgin Mary to receive now the entire and full right of disposing of these goods according to God's holy will. May she cast out any and all evil spirits, sanctify our goods, protect them from any future evil action, and use them for the glory of God.

I, _____, a faithless sinner, renew and ratify today the vows of my Baptism; I renounce forever Satan, his pomps and works; and I give myself entirely to Jesus Christ, the Incarnate Wisdom, to carry my cross after Him all the days of my life, and to be more faithful to Him than I have ever been before. In the presence of all the heavenly court I choose you, the Mother of God, this day for my Mother and Mistress. I deliver and consecrate to you, as your servant, my body and soul, my goods, both interior and exterior, and even the value of all my good actions, past, present and future; leaving to you the entire and full right of disposing of me, and all that belongs to me, without exception, according to your good pleasure, for the greater glory of God in time and in eternity. Amen.

[Adapted from St. Louis de Montfort's Consecration to Mary]

[If a priest is present add the following:]
Priest: *In the Most Holy Name of Jesus, by the authority of my priesthood, I invoke the keys of St. Peter and I ratify your*

breaking of each and every financial, business, and property curse and all curses coming against you and your family affecting your livelihood, your property, your finances or any goods or any works. With that same authority, in Jesus' name, I bind any evil spirits that may have attached themselves to you or harass you in any way as a result of these curses and I command them to leave you now and go immediately and directly to the foot of the cross for our Lord Jesus to deal with as he wills. Vade Retro Satanas. In the name of Jesus Christ leave them now. + Father, Son and Holy Spirit. Amen

THREE R'S
FOR CASTING OUT DEMONS

To "renounce" is to give back any benefits desired or received in the demonic relationship.

To "reject" is to make an act of the will which says in effect: "I do not want this evil spirit."

To "rebuke" is sharply denouncing the evil spirit.

In deliverance work, an important step in the process of liberation is completely cutting the relationship between the individual and the evil spirit.

In the Holy Name of Jesus, I renounce, I reject, and I rebuke the spirit of _____ [3X]

I bind and cast out all aforementioned evil spirits from me sending them to the foot of the Cross of my Lord and Savior, Jesus Christ, for Him to do with as He wills and to never return to me again. [SMC staff]

PRAYER TO BREAK
THE FREEMASONIC AND OTHER
OCCULT CURSES

(Abbreviated Short Form)

Our Father, Creator of heaven and earth, I come to you in the name of Jesus Christ your Son. I come as a sinner seeking forgiveness and cleansing from all sins committed against you, and others made in your image. I honor my earthly father and mother and all of my ancestors of flesh and blood, and of the spirit by adoption and godparents, but I utterly turn away from and renounce all their sins. I forgive all my ancestors for the effects of their sins on [my children and] me. I confess and renounce all of my own sins. I renounce and rebuke Satan and every spiritual power of his affecting my family and me.

I renounce and forsake all involvement in Freemasonry or any other lodge or craft or occult organization by my ancestors and myself. I renounce witchcraft, the principal spirit behind Freemasonry, and I renounce Baphomet (and Asmodeus), the Spirit of the Antichrist and the curse of the Luciferian doctrine. I renounce the idolatry, blasphemy, secrecy and deception of Masonry at every level. I specifically renounce the insecurity, the love of position and power, the love of money, avarice or greed, and the pride that would have led my ancestors into Masonry.

I renounce every position held in the lodge by any of my ancestors, including "Master," "Worshipful Master" or any other. I renounce the calling of any man 'Master' for Jesus Christ is my only master and Lord. I ask humbly for the blood of Jesus Christ, your Son, to cleanse me and my family from all these sins I have confessed and renounced, to cleanse my spirit, my soul, my mind, my emotions and every part of my body which has been affected by these sins. In Jesus' name.

I renounce every evil spirit associated with Masonry, Witchcraft and all other sins. I command in the name of Jesus Christ for Satan and every evil spirit to be bound and to leave me and my family now, touching or harming no-one, and go to the place appointed for you by the Lord Jesus, never to return to me or my family. I ask to be delivered of every spirit of sickness, infirmity, curse, affliction, addiction, disease or allergy associated with these sins I have confessed and renounced. I surrender to God's Holy Spirit and to no other spirit all the places in my life where these sins have been. I ask you, Lord, to baptize me in your Holy Spirit. I take to myself the whole armor of God in accordance with Ephesians Chapter Six and rejoice in its protection as Jesus surrounds me and fills me with His Holy Spirit. I enthrone you, Lord Jesus, in my heart, for you are my Lord and my Savior, the source of eternal life. Thank you, amen.

[Adapted from Fr. Winston Cabading, "Catholic Handbook of Prayers for Spiritual Liberation and Exorcisms With Redactor's Notes," 2nd ed., The University of Santo Tomas Publishing House, Manila, Philippines, 2024, pp. 35-42.]

A DELIVERANCE PRAYER
TO DEFEAT THE WORK OF SATAN

O Divine Eternal Father, in union with your Divine Son and the Holy Spirit, and through the Immaculate Heart of Mary, I beg you to destroy the power of the evil spirits affecting me (and my family) especially the evil spirits of: (name them silently or out loud). Cast them into the deepest recesses of hell and chain them there forever! Take possession of your Kingdom which you have created and which is rightfully yours. Heavenly Father, give us the reign of the Sacred Heart of Jesus and the Immaculate Heart of Mary. I repeat this prayer out of pure love for you with every beat of my heart and with every breath I take. Amen.

[Adapted from Fr. Jose Francisco C. Syquia, "Catholic Handbook of Deliverance Prayers," Rev. ed. with 12 new prayers, Makati City, PI: St. Pauls Philippines, 2014, pp. 178-179.]

DEEP SCRUB
WITH THE PRECIOUS BLOOD AND
THE FIRE OF THE HOLY SPIRIT

Heavenly Father, I ask that you pour out the Most Precious Blood of our Lord Jesus right now upon me. I ask that the Most Precious Blood would flood my memory, imagination, emotions, common sense power and cogitative power. I ask that these parts be completely flooded with the Most Precious Blood. In the Most Holy Name of Jesus and through the power of the Most Precious Blood, I bind any and all evil spirits that may have attached to these parts or oppress them in any way, and

I command you to leave me now and go straight to the foot of the cross. I again flood these parts with the Most Precious Blood and this time in the Name of Jesus and with the power of the Most Precious Blood I destroy any structures in the parts established by evil spirits. I destroy these structures individually and separately and I dissolve them in the Most Precious Blood. I call upon the Fire of the Holy Spirit right now to go through my memory, imagination, emotions, common sense power and cogitative power. I ask that the Fire of Holy Spirit bring healing to these parts, to purify them, sanctify them and connect them to Our Lord Jesus.

I now ask the Most Precious Blood of our Lord Jesus to go to my heart. I completely flood my heart now with the Most Precious Blood. If any evil spirits have attached themselves to my heart or oppress it any way, I bind you now and command you in the name of Jesus and through the power of the Most Precious Blood to leave me now and go directly to the foot of the cross. I again flood my heart with the Most Precious Blood and this time I destroy any structures established by evil spirits in my heart. I destroy them individually and separately and dissolve them in the Most Precious Blood. I call upon the Fire of the Holy Spirit to go into my heart and I ask the fire of the Holy Spirit to bring healing to my heart, to heal it, purify it, sanctify it and connect it with the Sacred Heart of Jesus.

I now ask the Most Precious Blood to go through each of the five senses, both interior and exterior senses of sight, hearing, smell, touch and taste. I completely flood these senses with the Most Precious Blood. In the Most Holy

Name of Jesus I bind any evil spirits that may have attached to or oppress the senses in any way and through the power of the Most Precious Blood and Holy Name of Jesus I command you to leave me now and go directly to the foot of the cross. I again flood these senses with the Most Precious Blood and this time I destroy any and all structures established by demons in these senses. I destroy these structures individually and separately and dissolve them in the Most Precious Blood. I call upon the Fire of the Holy Spirit to go through these senses right now. And I ask that the Fire of the Holy Spirit heal these senses, purify them, sanctify them and connect them with our Lord Jesus.

I ask Father that you give me the mind of Jesus and his heart. Give me the eyes of our Lord, the ears, the nose, the mouth and tongue, the hands and feet of our Lord. Configure me to the Sacred Heart of your Son Jesus.

I now ask that the Most Precious Blood of Our Lord Jesus would go through the entire nervous system. I ask that it would go from the front of my brain to the back of the brain, down my spine and out to every nerve of my body. I completely flood the nervous system again and again and again. In the Most Holy Name of Jesus and through the power of His Most Precious Blood I bind any evil spirits who may be attached to my nervous system or oppress it in any way. I command you to leave me now and go straight to the foot of the Cross. I again flood the nervous system with the Most Precious Blood and this time I destroy any structures established by evil spirits to use against me. I destroy these structures collectively and individually, and dissolve them with the

Most Precious Blood. In the Holy Name of Jesus, I call upon the Fire of the Holy Spirit right now to go through the nervous system, from the front of the brain, to the back of the brain, down the spine and out of every nerve of the body. I ask that the Fire of the Holy Spirit heal my nervous system, purify it, sanctify it, and connect it to Our Lord Jesus.

I now ask that the Most Precious Blood of Our Lord Jesus go through every organ and system of my body, from the top of the head down to the soles of the feet. I ask that it go through the respiratory system, circulatory system, digestive system, lymphatic system, immune system, endocrine system, reproductive system, skeletal system, through every muscle and fiber of my being. I flood them again and again and again. In the Most Holy Name of Jesus and through the power of His Most Precious Blood, I bind any evil spirits that may be attached to or oppress any organ or system of my body and I command you, in Jesus' name, to leave now and go to the foot of the Cross. Again I flood every system and organ of my body and this time I destroy any structures established by evil spirits to use against me, I destroy them individually and separately and I dissolve them in the Precious Blood of our Lord Jesus. I ask that the Fire of the Holy Spirit would come upon me now and go through every organ and system of my body, from top of my head to the soles of my feet. I ask that the Fire of the Holy Spirit would bring healing to these parts, that it would purify them, sanctify them and connect them with our Lord Jesus. In the name of Jesus, may I be healed. In the name of Jesus, may God give me peace. [SMC staff]

DELIVERANCE SESSION
FOR THE HOME

In the absence of a Catholic priest who would do the deliverance of the home, the Catholic family, united in the true faith, can do it for their own home.

Things needed:

- *Holy water*

- *Blessed Salt*

- *Blessed Incense and Incense charcoal (optional)*

- *Blessed Oil*

- *Blessed Candles*

- *Blessed Sacramentals (e.g. Crucifix, St. Benedict Medals, Holy Images)*

Important things to do:

- *A Catholic priest should bless the Holy water, Blessed Salt, Blessed incense, Blessed oil, Blessed Candles, and the Sacramentals.*

- *Every member of the household should go and make a good and holy confession of sins before a priest.*

- *They should attend Holy Mass and receive Holy Communion.*

- *Praying the Holy Rosary can precede the rite of deliverance. The rosary should be prayed reverently and devoutly.*

To be prayed by the head of the family or a member of the family—

The blessed candles can be lighted. Make the Sign of the Cross and say in faith:

In the name of the Father, and of the Son, and of the Holy Spirit. Amen.

Lord have mercy on us. Christ have mercy on us. Lord have mercy on us.

PRAYER

Lord, almighty, merciful and omnipotent God, Father, Son and Holy Spirit, drive out from me and my family all influence of evil spirits. Father, in the name of Jesus Christ, I plead you to break any chain that the Devil has on me and my family.

Pour upon us the most Precious Blood of your Son. May his sacred and redeeming blood break all bonds of our bodies or minds. I ask you this through the intercession of the Blessed Virgin Mary, of St. Joseph, St. Nicholas, St. Dominic, St. Thomas Aquinas and all the Saints and Holy Angels of God.

Archangels Michael, Gabriel, and Raphael, intercede and come to our help. Defend us from the Enemy of our Souls and salvation.

(Make the sign of the Cross)

In the name of Jesus, I command all demons that could have any influence over me and my family to leave us forever. By his scourging, his crown of thorns, his cross, by his blood and resurrection, I command all evil spirits to leave me and my family.

(Make the sign of the cross)

By the true God, by the Holy God, by God who can do all, in the name of Jesus, my Savior and Lord, leave me and my family. Amen.

HOLY WATER

While sprinkling Holy Water in the house and around the property, pray:

By the sprinkling of holy water, drive away from us O Lord, the power of the enemy and keep us your servants in peace and tranquility.

(Make the sign of the Cross)

In the name of the Father, and of the Son, and of the Holy Spirit. Amen. (*The prayer can be repeated until you have covered the whole property.*)

BLESSED SALT

Blessed salt can be used in those areas that holy water cannot reach.

By the sprinkling of this blessed salt, drive away from us O Lord, the power of the enemy and keep us your servants in peace and tranquility.

(Make the sign of the Cross)

In the name of the Father, and of the Son, and of the Holy Spirit. Amen. (*The prayer can be repeated until you have covered the whole property.*)

BLESSED INCENSE *(optional)*

Light a piece of the charcoal. Let it turn amber (all red) before putting in incense. And when putting incense and allowing its smoke to fill the room, pray:

By the lighting of this blessed incense, drive away from us, O Lord, the power of the enemy and keep us your servants in peace and tranquility.

(Make the sign of the Cross)

In the name of the Father, and of the Son, and of the Holy Spirit. Amen.

Then go around the house and backyard with the smoking incense as you pray:

Let our prayer rise before you like sweet smelling incense, O Lord. And by the smoke of this blessed incense drive away from us the power of the enemy and keep us your servants in peace and tranquility.

(Make the sign of the Cross)

In the name of the Father, and of the Son, and of the Holy Spirit. Amen.

(The prayer can be repeated until you have covered the whole property.)

BLESSED OIL

Dip your thumb in the blessed oil, and trace the sign of the cross on the doors and windows of the house, as you pray:

With the sign of your most holy cross and by this holy oil, drive away from us O Lord, the power of the enemy and keep us your servants in peace and tranquility. In the name of the *(Make the sign of the Cross)* Father, and of the Son, and of the Holy Spirit. Amen. *(The prayer can be repeated until you have covered the whole property.)*

Afterwards, gather in the main room of the house, and offer the prayer:

Eternal rest grant unto the faithful departed, O Lord. And let perpetual light shine upon them.

May they rest in your peace. Amen.

May the souls of the faithful departed, through the mercy of God, rest in peace. Amen.

O my Jesus, forgive us our sins.
Save us from the fires of hell.
And lead all souls into heaven,
Especially those in need of your mercy. Amen

Our Father who art in heaven, hallowed be thy name. Thy kingdom come. Thy will be done on earth as it is in heaven. Give us this day our daily bread, and forgive us our trespasses, as we forgive those who trespass against us, and lead us not into temptation, but deliver us from evil. For thine is the kingdom, and the power, and the glory, for ever and ever. Amen.

Hail Mary, full of grace. The Lord is with thee. Blessed art thou among women, and blessed is the fruit of thy womb, Jesus. Holy Mary, Mother of God, pray for us sinners, now and at the hour of our death. Amen.

St. Michael the Archangel, defend us in battle. Be our defense against the wickedness and snares of the Devil. May God rebuke him, we humbly pray, and do thou, O Prince of the heavenly hosts, by the power of God, thrust into hell Satan, and all the evil spirits, who prowl about the world seeking the ruin of souls. Amen.

Glory be to the Father, and to the Son, and to the Holy Spirit. As it was in the beginning is now and will be forever. Amen.

(Make the sign of the Cross and say in faith)

In the name of the Father, and of the Son, and of the Holy Spirit. Amen.

Repeat the prayers and blessings when necessary every day as long as it is suspected that there is still an evil spirit lingering. In the case of severe demonic infestation of the house or property, the intervention of the Church through her priest is to be sought for.

Never use a talisman or anything from the occult or New Age. They may seem to heal or stop the evil presence. But in reality they make it worse because now the evil spirits enter your house waiting for the right time to do their evil work.

[adapted from Fr. Winston Cabading, "Catholic Handbook of Prayers for Spiritual Liberation and Exorcisms

With Redactor's Notes," 2nd ed., The University of Santo Tomas Publishing House, Manila, Philippines, 2024, pp. 327-332.]

A PARENT'S PRAYER

Spouses have divine authority over their own bodies, their spouses and their children who are minors. In that knowledge, this prayer has a parent invoking that authority and casting out demons and evil from them. For their adult children, they are invoking God to heal and liberate them.

Heavenly Father, I invoke the full authority you have given me as a spouse and a parent and I lift any curses, spells, seals, hexes, vexes, consecrations, voodoo, or any occult action or any evil affecting me or my spouse or my children who are minors. In Jesus' name, I cast out all evil spirits that are harming us. In Jesus' name, I reject them, I rebuke them, I renounce them, and I cast them out! For all my children, I beg you heavenly father to hear a parent's plea and free them from any of these occult actions or any evil, and cast out all evil spirits. Father, I beseech you to send a spirit of unity and peace to my family. Heal the divisions in our family; may those family members who are estranged from each other be reconciled in forgiveness and love. May we live together in your peace. I pray for special healing graces for each one of us. Heal the wounds that plague us—heal any depression, anxiety, fears, compulsions, addictions, angers, resentments, and any and all mental and physical illnesses. Restore us to full health. I especially ask for the following specific grace for my family, if it be your holy will *(here mention the specific intention silently or out loud)*.

Most of all, may you infuse into our hearts the gift of faith, always trusting in you. Bring back any of us who have wandered from the faith. May we be fully protected from all harm and evil by the Shield of Faith and the Sword of Truth. I make this parent's prayer in the holy name of Jesus begging the powerful intercession of the Holy Family with the Virgin Mary and St. Joseph, and all the saints. [SMC staff]

A SCRIPTURAL DELIVERANCE PRAYER

It is the Word of God that casts out the demons:

"Then the Lord God said to the snake; Because you have done this, cursed are you among all the animals ... On your belly you shall crawl, and dust you shall eat all the days of your life." Gen 3:14

Deliver us O Lord from all evil.

"How you have fallen from the heavens, O Morning Star, son of the dawn! How you have been cut down to the earth, you who conquered nations! In your heart you said: 'I will scale the heavens; Above the stars of God I will set up my throne ... ascend above the tops of the clouds; I will be like the Most High!' No! Down to Sheol you will be brought to the depths of the pit!" Is 14:12-15

Deliver us O Lord from all evil.

"Jesus said to him, 'Get away, Satan! It is written: The Lord your God shall your worship and him alone shall you serve.' Then the devil left him and, behold, angels came and ministered to him." Mt 4:10-11

Deliver us O Lord from all evil.

"A demoniac who could not speak was brought to Jesus, and when the demon was driven out the mute man spoke. The crowds were amazed." Mt 9:32-33

Deliver us O Lord from all evil.

"But if it by the Spirit of God that I drive out demons, then the kingdom of God has come upon you." Mt 12:28

Deliver us O Lord from all evil.

"'What have you to do with us, Jesus of Nazareth? Have you come to destroy us?'... Jesus rebuked him and said, 'Quiet! Come out of him!' The unclean spirit convulsed him and with a loud cry came out of him." Mk 1:24-26

Deliver us O Lord from all evil.

"No one can enter a strong man's house to plunder his property, unless he first ties up the strong man. Then he can plunder his house." Mk 3:27

Deliver us O Lord from all evil.

"They [Legion] pleaded with Jesus, 'Send us into the swine...' The unclean spirits came out, and entered the swine ... rushed down a steep bank into the sea, where they were drowned." Mk 5:12-13

Deliver us O Lord from all evil.

"Jesus summoned the Twelve and began to send them out...and gave them authority over unclean spirits... They drove out many demons." Mk 6:7,13

Deliver us O Lord from all evil.

"She [the Greek woman] begged Jesus to drive the demon out of her daughter. He said to her, ... 'it is not right to take the food of the children and throw it to the dogs.' 'Lord, even the dogs under the table eat the children's scraps.' Then he said to her, 'For this saying you may go; the demon has gone out of your daughter.'" Mk 7:26-29

Deliver us O Lord from all evil.

"Jesus rebuked the unclean spirit, and said to it, 'Mute and deaf spirit, I command you: come out of him and never enter him again.' Shouting and throwing the boy into convulsions, it came out." Mk 9:25-26

Deliver us O Lord from all evil.

"And if your eye causes you to sin, pluck it out. Better for you to enter into the kingdom of God with one eye than with two eyes be thrown into Gehenna, where 'their worm does not die, and the fire is not quenched.'" Mk 9:46-48

Deliver us O Lord from all evil.

"As Jesus was coming forward, the demon threw the boy to the ground in a convulsion; but Jesus rebuked the unclean spirit, healed the boy, and returned him to his father. And all were astonished." Lk 9:42-43

Deliver us O Lord from all evil.

"The seventy[-two] returned rejoicing, and said, 'Lord, even the demons are subject to us because of your name!' Jesus said, 'I have observed Satan fall like lightning from the sky. Behold, I have given you the power to tread ... upon the full force of the enemy; and nothing will harm you. Nevertheless do not rejoice because the spirits are subject to you but rejoice because your names are written in heaven." Lk 10:17-20

Deliver us O Lord from all evil.

"And a woman was there who for eighteen years had been crippled by a spirit; she was bent over...When Jesus saw her, he called to her and said, 'Woman, you are set free of your infirmity.' He laid his hands upon her and she at once stood straight up." Lk 13:11-13

Deliver us O Lord from all evil.

The Son of Man will send his angels, and they will collect out of his kingdom all who cause others to sin and all evildoers. They will throw them into the fiery furnace, where there will be wailing and grinding of teeth. Then the righteous will shine like the sun in the kingdom of their Father." Mt 13: 41-43

Deliver us O Lord from all evil.

"Whereas you are tormented. Moreover, between us and you a great chasm is established to prevent anyone from crossing ..." Lk 16:25-26

Deliver us O Lord from all evil.

"In the beginning was the Word, and the Word was with God, and the Word was God...The light shines in the darkness, and the darkness has not overcome it...And the Word became flesh and made his dwelling among us." Jn 1: 1,5,14

Deliver us O Lord from all evil.

"Holy Father...I guarded them, and none of them was lost except the son of destruction, in order that the Scripture might be fulfilled....I do not ask that you take them out of the world, but that you keep them from the evil one." Jn 17:12,15

Deliver us O Lord from all evil.

"Many signs and wonders were done among the people at the hands of the apostles...A large number of people from the towns in the vicinity of Jerusalem gathered, bringing the sick and those disturbed by unclean spirits, and they were all cured." Acts 5:12,16

Deliver us O Lord from all evil.

"When Simon the Magician saw that the Spirit was conferred by the laying on of the apostles' hands, he offered them money and said, 'Give me this power too...' But Peter said to him, 'May your money perish with you... Repent of this wickedness of yours ...For I see that you are filled with bitter gall and in the bonds of iniquity.' Simon the Magician said in reply, 'Pray for me to the

Lord, that nothing of what you have said may come upon me.'" Acts 8:18-24

Deliver us O Lord from all evil.

"We met a slave girl with an oracular spirit, who used to bring a large profit to her owners through her fortune-telling. She began to follow Paul and us, shouting, 'These people are slaves of the Most High God, who proclaim to you a way of salvation.' ... Paul said to the spirit, "I command you in the name of Jesus Christ to come out of her.' Then it came out at that moment." Acts 16:16-18

Deliver us O Lord from all evil.

"They were all amazed and said to one another, 'What is there about his word? For with authority and power he commands the unclean spirits, and they come out." Lk 4:36

Deliver us O Lord from all evil.

"War broke out in heaven; Michael and his angels battled against the dragon. The dragon and its angels fought back, but they did not prevail and there was no longer any place for them in heaven. The huge dragon, the ancient serpent...was thrown down to the earth... Then I heard a loud voice in heaven say: 'Now have salvation and power come, and the kingdom of our God and the authority of his Anointed. For the accuser of our brothers is cast out... They conquered him by the blood of the lamb." Rev 12:7-11

Deliver us O Lord from all evil.

Let us pray. Heavenly Father, in the Word made flesh, we witness Your Divine power to bind the Evil One and to cast him out. We give great thanks that Your Divine Son has given this same power to the Apostles. As we read the Scriptures and invoke the Word made flesh, may Christ's saving power once more be made manifest, the Spirit of God come upon us, the blood of the Lamb wash over us, and we be delivered from all evil.

CLEANSING PRAYER

Lord Jesus, thank you for sharing with us Your wonderful ministry of healing and deliverance. Thank you for the healing we have seen and experienced today. But we realize that the sickness and evil we encountered are more than our humanity can bear. So, cleanse us of any sadness, negativity, or despair that we may have picked up during the course of this ministry.

If our ministry has tempted us to anger, impatience, or lust, cleanse us of those temptations and replace them with love, joy and peace. If any evil spirits have attached themselves to us or oppress us in any way, spirits of earth, air, fire, or water, of the netherworld or of nature, and all spirits not of the Holy Spirit, we pray that these evil spirits would depart now and go straight to Jesus Christ, for Him to deal with as He wills.

Come, Holy Spirit, renew us, fill us anew with Your power, love and joy. Strengthen us where we have felt weak and clothe us with Your light. Fill us with life. And Lord Jesus, please send your holy angels to minister to us and our families and to guard and protect us from all sickness, harm, and accidents [and guard us on a safe trip home], and grant us a peaceful night's rest. We praise You now and forever.

Heavenly Father, in the Name of Jesus Christ our Lord and Savior, by the power of the Holy Spirit, we pray that the cleansing power of the precious blood of Your Son come upon us right now.

Purify us and wash us clean with the blood of Jesus from the top of our heads down to the very soles of our feet. Let this blood penetrate the very marrow of our bones to cleanse us from any entanglement from whatever evil spirits we have come in contact with during the course of our intercession.

Anoint us with the gifts of the Holy Spirit and refresh our body, soul, and spirit, and may the sign of Your holy cross drive away all evil spirits from us.

In the Name of the Father + and the Son and of the Holy Spirit. Amen.

[Fr. Winston Cabading, "Catholic Handbook of Prayers for Spiritual Liberation and Exorcisms With Redactor's Notes," 1st ed., The University of Santo Tomas Publishing House, Manila, Philippines, 2016, pp. 212-213.]

Endnotes

1 Saint Gemma Galgani, *The Saint Gemma Galgani Collection* [4 books], Kindle version, p. 85 of 544.

2 St. Faustina, *Diary of Saint Maria Faustina Kowalska: Divine Mercy In My Soul,"* Kindle, Notebook II, p. 264.

3 St. Faustina, *Diary of Saint Maria Faustina Kowalska: Divine Mercy In My Soul,"* Kindle, Notebook II, p. 213.

4 Catherine of Siena, *The Dialogue: A Treatise of Discretion*, Kindle, p. 56 of 169, #46.

5 *Protection, binding and cleansing prayers can all be found on our app: "Catholic Exorcism" or on our website: www.catholicexorcism.org*

6 St. Catherine of Siena, **The Dialogue of Saint Catherine of Siena**, Kindle, p. 131 of 169.

7 Philip Kosloski, "When Padre Pio was visited by a soul from purgatory," *Aleteia*, 11/07/17.

8 See "St. Louis-Marie de Montfort Total Consecration to Jesus through Mary," http://www.quies.org/True-Consecration-33-Day.pdf, accessed 2/12/23.

9 Satan does not have a body and thus cannot actually have physical sex with someone. However, Satan and demons can stimulate someone's mind so they have the experience of a sexual encounter with demons. It will feel very real to them.

10 See: Stephen J. Rossetti, *Diary of An American Exorcist: Demons, Possession, and the Modern-Day Battle against Ancient Evil*, Sophia Institute Press, Manchester, N.H., 2021, p. 107.

11 A definition of gaslighting: "psychological manipulation of a person usually over an extended period of time that causes the victim to question the validity of their own thoughts, perception of reality, or memories and typically leads to confusion, loss of confidence and self-esteem, uncertainty of one's emotional or mental stability, and a dependency on the perpetrator." See: https://www.merriam-webster.com/dictionary/gaslighting, accessed 2/4/25.

12 I know of at least two other exorcism teams in the USA and abroad that also report receiving demonic texts (see: https://newsinfo.inquirer.net/1354888/demonic-texts-the-enemy-can-use-technology-says-exorcist, accessed 2/4/25).

It is interesting and affirming that when speaking to exorcists around the globe how similar our experiences.

13   If the laity wish to recite such a prayer, we recommend they amend it to being a deprecatory prayer. Instead of directly commanding the demons to leave (an imperative prayer), the prayer would be addressed to God, Jesus, the Virgin Mary or some saints and angels. A deprecatory prayer asks them to cast out the demons.

14   The Spanish bishops put out a document November 2024 "His Mercy Extends from Generation to Generation" which made some important theological distinctions including that future generations are not culpable for previous generation's sins.

15   Holly Meyer, "Nearly 7 in 10 U.S. adults believe in angels, AP-NORC poll finds," PBS News online, Jul 29, 2023. https://www.pbs.org/newshour/nation/nearly-7-in-10-u-s-adults-believe-in-angels-ap-norc-poll-finds, accessed 2/4/25.

16   Charles Fraune, "*Slaying Dragons II-The Rise of the Occult,*" Kindle, chpt 8, loc. 2135 of 7899.

17   Ibid., chpt 8, loc. 2247 of 7899.

18   Sister Emmanuel Maillard, "*Maryam of Bethlehem, The Little Arab,*" Kindle, Children of Medjugorje, Inc., 2020, pp. 60-66.

19   Father Carl Vogl, "*Begone Satan: A Soul Stirring Account of an Exorcism in Earling, Iowa in 1928,*" Kindle, p. 21.

20   All three of these extended case studies are used with the express, written permission of the afflicted persons. Each of them wanted to share their stories so that others could learn from them and not become involved in such evil and destructive practices. I thank them for their generosity and their ministry to others.

21   All excerpts used with the woman's permission.

22   *JR Illustrations of Human Effigies in Tibetan Ritual Texts: With Remarks on Specific Anatomical Figures and Their Possible Iconographic Source. BRYAN J. CUEVAS. AS, Series 3*, 21, 1 (2011), pp. 73-97 C The Royal Asiatic Society 2011 doi:10.1017/S1356186310000611

23   All excerpts used with the woman's permission.

24   All excerpts used with "Juan's" permission.